T. Hall Caine

Sonnets of Three Centuries

A Selection Including Many Examples hitherto Unpublished

T. Hall Caine

Sonnets of Three Centuries
A Selection Including Many Examples hitherto Unpublished

ISBN/EAN: 9783337275143

Printed in Europe, USA, Canada, Australia, Japan

Cover: Foto ©Thomas Meinert / pixelio.de

More available books at **www.hansebooks.com**

SONNETS

OF

THREE CENTURIES

SONNETS

OF

THREE CENTURIES:

A SELECTION

INCLUDING

MANY EXAMPLES HITHERTO UNPUBLISHED.

EDITED BY T. HALL CAINE.

LONDON:
ELLIOT STOCK, 62 PATERNOSTER ROW.
1882.

CONTENTS.

PREFACE.

T will readily be seen that the plan of this book is unlike anything hitherto adopted in any similar anthology. The aim has been to represent within the limits of a quintessential selection the whole body of native sonnet literature down to our own time. Those who know the subject will perceive that numbers of inedited examples have been collected from obscure sources. It will be seen that as many as a dozen sonnet-writers, who have never before been omitted from a volume of this kind, have not found a place within these pages; but it cannot escape observation that fully forty poets, in the course of the three centuries compassed by the compilation, have here for the first time been included. By the kindness of living poets of established rank it has also been possible very greatly to enhance the interest of the collection, by the addition of a body of sonnets never hitherto published. For this exceptional attraction gratitude from the editor to those who have afforded him disinterested help is due.

The primary purpose has been to make a representative selection such as may afford a complete view of the history and growth of a form of verse now much in favour and requisition; and especially, by a liberal and impartial selection from the sonnets of contemporary writers, of every style and school, to show clearly what is now the character of the sonnet in the present stage of our literature. Metrical and chronological indices, and historical, explanatory, and analytical notes, will be found appended to the volume, and these, together with the textual rendering and arrangement adopted, may prove helpful in the way of critical elucidation. But it is hoped that the book may be acceptable not only to students of the sonnet, but to all lovers of whatever is beautiful in English sonnet poetry. To this end an endeavour has been made to secure as much variety in subject-matter as seemed consistent with a selection whereof the first elective test required that each example have intrinsic value; and to bring together within reasonable limits as many pieces as by contrast appeared to illustrate the methods of different masters in the treatment of similar themes. All systematic collocation of kindred examples must, however, remain with the reader as a task. The arrangement adopted in this volume is of necessity purely chronological.

It were scarcely rash to hope that a book compiled upon principles so catholic and from sources so inexhaustible, can hardly be opened on any page of the text without being found to contain something able to lighten and beguile the moments of all to whom English poetry is anything. But while the sonnets are so chosen as to appeal to a wide circle, it cannot be expected that the remainder of this preface will be found interesting to more than a few readers; yet to the limited company addressed the matter dealt with must be one of enduring moment. It constitutes an argument going to show the legitimacy and purity of the English sonnet, as against the allegation that our sonnet literature is a bastard outcome of the Italian.

We hear it so constantly asserted that the sonnet in England is a naturalised form of verse, that we seem to have begun to grant the statement an unquestioning assent. As a result of this, we are compelled to resort to specious expedients by way of explanation when we find ourselves face to face with the great body of English sonnets, and perceive that only a small proportion bears an affinity to what is accepted as the original code. Of course the error involved comes of begging the question, and only requires to be challenged to succumb. Thereupon, it is seen that in the sonnet our literature possesses of its own right a species of poetry as beautiful and perfect as indigenous. The facts are well known and easily traversed. The word SONNET (literally *a little strain*) was first employed by the very early Italian writers to denote simply a short poem limited to the exposition of a single idea, sentiment, or emotion; two notable instances in point occur in Dante's *Vita Nuova*.[1] Gradually it became confined in its application to a lyric of fourteen lines, constructed variously as to scheme of rhyme, and subject to no arbitrary rules as to development of thought. Finally, the name

[1] In Petrarch it may be noted that there occur among the sonnets some exceptional pieces of fourteen lines, which he, presumably, would have classed as sonnets, but which are of the *Ballata* character. A more minute reference to such points in Petrarch and earlier Italian poets will be found in the indices of forms.

became exclusively associated with a form of verse affording a prescribed presentment of idea and metre. Now, when the word SONNET was first employed in England, it was used in its simple sense, and there seems to be some difficulty in discovering at what period it ceased to bear its literal application. It is true that Sir Thomas Wyat, upon returning from Italy, wrote a few poems, apparently in imitation of certain features of the method of Petrarch, and to these the name of Sonnets was attached. The following is the most notable example:—

Farëwell, Love, and all thy laws for ever!
Thy baited hooks shall tangle me no more:
Senec and Plato call me from thy lore
To perfect wealth my wit for to endeavour.
In blind error when I did persévêr,
Thy sharp repulse, that pricketh aye so sore,
Taught me in trifles that I set no store;
But 'scaped forth thence, since, liberty is lever.
Therefore, farewell! go trouble younger hearts,
And in me claim no more authority:
With idle youth go use thy property,
And thereon spend thy many brittle darts;
For hitherto though I have lost my time,
Me list no longer rotten boughs to climb.

But no definite direction appears to have been given to sonnet literature by this partial imitation of Italian models. Contemporaneously with Wyat, the Earl of Surrey produced poems constructed upon the model subsequently known as Shakspearean; and, following Surrey, Spenser wrote a series similar in scheme and scope, but with a variation in the arrangement of rhymes. Meantime, poems characterised by measureless variety of structure were by these poets and their contemporaries denominated sonnets. Down to Spenser, therefore, no deliberative effort appears to have been made to naturalise any specific form of the Italian sonnet, and hence the limitation sometimes observed as to number and length of lines must have been accepted merely for disciplinarian purposes, in order to curb the insatiate demand for room, which was then, as it is now, the mark of a restless intellect. No consistent or sustained endeavour was made to obey the approved Italian code as to structure, and this, probably, was because the genius of our language did not demand such obedience. The rule which Petrarch had established of at least four different rhyme-sounds in the sonnet may have seemed to the early English sonnet-writers, as it did afterwards to Coleridge, to have arisen from the desire the Italians had to have as many as four rhymes within a space in which there might naturally occur no more than two, inasmuch as the great and grievous defect of their language is a sameness in the final sound of its words. In the choice of a more varied rhyme-scheme the English poets may indeed have been influenced by a belief that it would be ridiculous to make the defect of a foreign language a reason for their not availing themselves of a marked excellency of their own. Apart, however, from all regard for structural divergence, we have merely to set side by side the intellectual plotting of a sonnet by Petrarch and that of a sonnet by Spenser, to see clearly that this form of verse in England is a distinct growth. In the one we perceive a conscious centralisation of some idea systematically subdivided, with each of its parts allotted a distinctive place, so that to dislodge anything would be to destroy the whole. In the other we recognise a facet of an idea or sentiment so presented as to work up from concrete figure to abstract application. The one constitutes a rounded unity, the other is a development; the one is thrown off at the point at which it has become quintessential and a thing in itself, the other is still in process of evolution.

We require clearly to see first that the very early Italians themselves sometimes (though rarely) used the term SONNET in all its literal breadth of application, and next, that the first English writers who appropriated the name made no conscious effort of consequence to imitate the more approved archetypal pattern, before we approach the sonnets of Shakspeare in a temper that permits us to perceive wherein they constitute a native outcome of unsurpassable excellence and unimpeachable purity. A peculiar adaptability of language to vehicle is then seen to establish for the Shakspearean model the character of a perfect English sonnet. The metrical structure is plainly determined by the intellectual modelling. Let us therefore set ourselves to consider what constitutes the function the Shakspearean sonnet fulfils. The thing that first strikes us is that the thought, as a whole, is of the nature of an applied symbol. Then we see that it does not in the English, as in the Italian form, fall asunder like the acorn into unequal parts of a perfect organism, but is sustained without break until it reaches a point at which a personal appropriation needs to be made. Finally, we perceive that the ultimate application (which was also the primary purpose) consolidates the thought, and gives it a separate and unified entity. We obtain a full view of this by careful analysis of any representative example. Let us examine the intellectual, emotional, and metrical structure of the sonnet on lust :—

The expense of spirit in a waste of shame
  Is lust in action ; and till action, lust
Is perjured, murderous, bloody, full of blame,
  Savage, extreme, rude, cruel, not to trust ;
Enjoyed no sooner but despisèd straight ;
  Past reason hunted ; and no sooner had,
Past reason hated, as a swallowed bait
  On purpose laid to make the taker mad :
Mad in pursuit, and in possession so ;
  Had, having, and in quest to have, extreme ;
A bliss in proof, and proved, a very woe ;
  Before, a joy proposed ; behind, a dream.
All this the world well knows ; yet none knows well
To shun the heaven that leads men to this hell.

First seizing the representative points of a noble idea, Shakspeare in this sonnet goes on from line to line begetting thought out of thought, kindling image out of image ; yet the whole gravitates about a central scheme, and the meaning is all inwoven. Here there is no distinct plotting of thought, no systematic placing of proportionated ideas, no building up to definite point other than that indicated at the outset. Where, at the ninth line, the thought appears to take a fresh departure such as is nearly always observable in sonnets by Petrarch, it is really doing no more than evolve a new aspect out of the old one. Clearly there is no other form of verse that could have been made to serve so well the uses herein compassed. The stanza did not exist that could have embraced the whole business of the first twelve lines. The nature of the thought and its method of development (covering the growth of the idea from prologue to epilogue) forbade attempt at rounded unity of presentment. It made demand of a measure linking passage to passage, not compelling a focused centralisation whereof the first word should foretell the last. A succession of decasyllabic couplets kneaded in Shakspeare's hands would doubtless have answered a similar end, but it is proof of the purity and perfectness of the Shakspearean sonnet that couplets could not have been employed. By their use the emphasis and rest of the close would have been sacrificed. No form, obviously, but that of three interlacing English quatrains of alternate-rhyming lines followed, after a pause, by a couplet, could have afforded an adequate realisation of the English idea embodied. So absolutely is this so of a representative sonnet, that it were hardly rash to say that the sonnet by Shakspeare does not exist in which the structure of thought would allow of Petrarchian treatment. The reason is not far to seek. The mind of the Italian poet was wont to hold itself at poise above a thought, revolving it inwardly until the primary uncertain outlines took consistent shape and craved balanced utterance. The mind of the English poet seized as they arose the thronging hints of an idea, and cast them forth one after one in the first beauty of conception, and knitted them into harmonious theme only in a final word of condensed application. And what is true of Petrarch is true of the bias of the whole Italian intellect; and what is true of Shakspeare is true of the bias of the whole English intellect. Hence the Shakspearean sonnet is distinctly the sonnet of the English mind and tongue, and must not be regarded as metrically an irregular outcome of the Petrarchian sonnet, to which, as we see, it bears not the remotest affinity of intellectual design. The relative excellence of the two models involves other considerations. All that is now necessary to establish is that the Shakspearean sonnet is wholly indigenous and, within itself, entirely pure.

A glance at the metrical indices which may be found at the close of this volume will readily show how desirable it is to redeem our sonnet literature from the unmerited reproach of illegitimacy. Therein it will be seen that a great body of English sonnets are cast in the English form with which Shakspeare's name is associated, and that many of the noblest extant examples could not exist apart from it. The variation in the scheme of rhyme is the least point of divergence from the archetypal pattern, and seems to have been rendered necessary equally by the paucity of rhyme-words in our language and by the essential difference in the intellectual structure adopted. The radical distinction lies in the building of the thought, and this justifies all lesser differences.

And now that we have at least challenged an error of critical verdict relating to Shakspeare, it seems necessary to make effort to disturb an error of ascription concerning Milton. It is not more frequently maintained that the sonnets of the one are irregular, than that those of the other are perfect examples designed to vindicate the possibilities of the Italian sonnet in English.

In saying that Milton's sonnet work signalised a return to the original code, we have hitherto been led astray by cursory observation of the mere arrangement of his rhymes. Milton's sonnets, like Shakspeare's, are essentially English in all that constitutes their fundamental character. Points of departure from the primary English structure, however, Milton did initiate, and the full sum of gain and loss involved may be seen by technical analysis of that most memorable utterance which concentrates the varied excellences and defects of his sonnet muse.

Avenge, O Lord, thy slaughtered saints, whose bones
  Lie scattered on the Alpine mountains cold;
  Even them who kept thy truth so pure of old,
When all our fathers worshipped stocks and stones,
Forget not: in thy book record their groans
  Who were thy sheep, and in their ancient fold
  Slain by the bloody Piemontese, that rolled
Mother with infant down the rocks. Their moans
The vales redoubled to the hills, and they
  To Heaven. Their martyred blood and ashes sow
O'er all the Italian fields, where still doth sway
  The triple Tyrant; and from these may grow
A hundredfold, who having learnt thy way,
  Early may fly the Babylonian woe.

Setting aside the august conception generated by this majestic invocation, and addressing ourselves dispassionately to the observation of its artistic qualities, we first perceive that the rhyme scheme of the sonnet yields obedience to the rigid Petrarchian rule, demanding four different sounds. Beyond this no canon of art peculiar to the approved Italian pattern has been regarded. Indeed the essential part of the code has been violated. But what is the value of the concession? Are the potentialities of the Italian sonnet in our language triumphantly displayed? Surely not so. Milton wrote no more than eighteen English sonnets, and were they all faultless examples, being so few, the possibilities of the original structure would not be assured. When a great poet, following in his steps, made effort to imitate his form of sonnet, the all but insurmountable difficulty of doing so continuously and under every condition of impulse became apparent. After a single experimental effort, Wordsworth's early sonnets were in all respects counterparts to Milton's, but the great body of his later sonnet writings display a preponderating percentage which must be pronounced irregular if judged of by Milton's standard. Nor can the few examples Milton himself achieved be considered free from marks of the mischief induced by working in unwonted fetters. The grievous technical blemish of the sonnet just quoted is, that the vowel sounds of the rhyme words are throughout uniform, and that, consequently, the sensitive ear is from first to last deprived of the grateful sense of flow and ebb of melody which the alternate open and close vowels afford. Moreover, that Milton never made conscious endeavour to imitate the Petrarchian model becomes apparent by observation of his Italian sonnets, for in them the rhyme arrangement, though usually accurate at the beginning, is invariably faulty at the end. Whilst similar to the English examples in intellectual design, they are all, excepting two, yet nearer akin to the native form in closing with a couplet. The essential point of Milton's departure from the original code, however, is of more consequence than mere technical divergence, and lies in the radical structure of his sonnet-thought. A metrical subdivision into octave and sestet he certainly observes, and in this particular gravitates by force of instinct towards the method of the Italian poets, but no corresponding or answering intellectual and emotional subdivision is in his work ever aimed at. Octave flows into sestet without break of music or thought, which are sustained in one long breath from the first syllable to the last. This circumstance should itself serve as a satisfying refutation of those writers who, without reflection, go on asserting time after time that the potentialities of the Italian structure in English were by Milton first signalised and maintained. The clear truth that certain earlier poets who wrote exclusively in the Shakspearean form came, consciously or unconsciously, into closer accord with the canon requiring a subdivision of thought and melody, may be seen by setting side by side with the sonnet by Milton, already quoted, the following by Drayton, on lovers parting :—

Since there 's no help, come let us kiss and part,—
   Nay I have done, you get no more of me ;
And I am glad, yea, glad with all my heart,
   That thus so cleanly I myself can free ;
Shake hands for ever—cancel all our vows—
   And when we meet at any time again,
Be it not seen in either of our brows
   That we one jot of former love retain.

Now at the last gasp of Love's latest breath,
  When, his pulse failing, Passion speechless lies,
When Faith is kneeling by his bed of death,
  And Innocence is closing up his eyes,—
Now if thou would'st, when all have given him over,
From death to life thou might'st him yet recover.

Here are seen two facets of a sentiment, each as distinct from the other as the unequal parts of an acorn, and yet as indissolubly united beneath the amalgamating shell of a single, rounded, and perfected conception. Drayton never repeated the scheme, nor is it certain that any Shakspearean sonnet-writer consciously employed it, and the example is quoted in this connection with no other purpose than to show that so far from imitating the foreign model, Milton was behind other poets in appropriation of its salient feature of design, and thus to disturb the popular ascription to Milton of a desire deliberately to vindicate the Italian sonnet in England.

What may with unerring accuracy be ascribed to Milton is a desire to vindicate the *English* sonnet in England. His method of thought is such as has ever been native in our literature. Notwithstanding the rhetorical element interfused, his sonnet work has little in common with that of the poets who approached this form of verse fresh from the schools of the rhetoricians. Milton is throughout faithful to his English intellect, and his sonnets are, in the main, such as Shakspeare himself might have conceived, less much wealth of symbolic invention, and with an added weight and mass of diction. In tracing, therefore, the development of the sonnet in our language, what remains to be tabulated as Milton's ultimate contribution is an arrangement of rhyme which, in the hands of a master, lends itself to a mighty sweep of music, an abandonment of all point and climax, an effort after singleness of effect.

Within the lines of Shakspeare and of Milton all foremost sonnet-writers down to our own day have been content to work: on the one hand, Drayton, Coleridge, Hood, W. C. Roscoe, Tennyson-Turner; on the other, Wordsworth and Elizabeth Barrett Browning. Keats, indeed, who employed both English methods, seemed scarcely satisfied with either, and produced examples that unite certain of the cardinal virtues of each.

And now in our time the English sonnet has taken a new direction, acquired an enlarged significance, a broader mission; and to such circumstance is clearly due the marked preference for this vehicle which has been shown by some poets whose vocation does not appear primarily to lie within the domain of verse requiring before all things emphasis and condensation. When we set ourselves to investigate the developed type, we perceive that in the main it constitutes a return to the Petrarchian pattern, prompted, however, by other purposes, and achieving other results. Its governing constituents may be speedily traversed.

The quality that gave vividness and pungency to the Shakspearean sonnet was, that in the closing couplet the subject was capable of rising to a climax; the defect of the form lay in the tendency of the two last lines to produce the dubious effect of repercussion. The conspicuous beauty of the Miltonic form has been well described by Sir Henry Taylor as the absence of point in the evolution of the idea, whose peculiar charm lay in its being thrown off like a rocket, breaking into light and falling in a soft shower of brightness. The characteristic excellence of the contemporary type is distinct from both of these. Its merit and promise of enduring popularity consist in its being grounded in a fixed law of nature. The natural phenomenon it reproduces is the familiar one of the flow and ebb of a wave of the sea. The properties of the new model are illustrated in a sonnet by Mr. Theodore Watts, in which scholastic definition is happily blended with poetic fervour.

THE SONNET'S VOICE.

A METRICAL LESSON BY THE SEA-SHORE.

Yon silvery billows breaking on the beach
  Fall back in foam beneath the star-shine clear,
  The while my rhymes are murmuring in your ear
A restless lore like that the billows teach;
For on these sonnet-waves my soul would reach
  From its own depths, and rest within you, dear,
  As, through the billowy voices yearning here
Great Nature strives to find a human speech.

A sonnet is a wave of melody:
  From heaving waters of the impassioned soul
  A billow of tidal music one and whole
Flows in the 'octave'; then, returning free,
  Its ebbing surges in the 'sestet' roll
Back to the deeps of Life's tumultuous sea.[1]

[1] *The Athenæum*, September 17th, 1881.

Here it is seen that the 'sonnet-wave'—twofold in quality as well as movement—embraces flow and ebb of thought or sentiment, and flow and ebb of music. For the perfecting of a poem on this pattern the primary necessity, therefore, is, that the thought chosen be such as falls naturally into unequal parts, each essential to each, and the one answering the other. The first and fundamental part shall have unity of sound no less than unity of emotion, while in the second part the sonnet shall assume a freedom of metrical movement analogous to the lawless ebb of a returning billow. The sonnet-writer who has capacity for this structure may be known by his choice of theme. Instinctively or consciously he alights on subjects that afford this flow and ebb of emotion. Nor does he fail to find in every impulse animating his muse something that corresponds with the law of movement that governs the sea. We might instance Wordsworth's sonnet 'On the Extinction of the Venetian Republic,' and his 'It is a Beauteous Evening,' Keats's 'Chapman's Homer,' Leigh Hunt's 'Nile,' and amongst the sonnets of contemporary poets, W. B. Scott's 'Universe Void,' M. Arnold's 'Worldly Place,' D. G. Rossetti's 'Stillborn Love' and 'Lost Days,' A. C. Swinburne's 'Let us go forth,' Mathilde Blind's 'The Dead,' E. W. Gosse's 'Sophocles,' P. B. Marston's 'Desolate,' J. Payne's 'On Vaughan's Sacred Poems,' J. A. Symonds's 'To the Genius of Eternal Slumber,' E. Dowden's 'The Singer.' All this seems to signalise a return to the Petrarchian pattern, but is nevertheless indicative of a fuller development of the English model. The difference is radical. The Italian form demands two parts to the sonnet-thought, but they are as the two parts of an acorn; the later English form requires also two sides to the sonnet-thought, but they are as the two movements of a wave. In the one, the parts are separate and contrasted, yet united; in the other, they are blended, the same in substance, distinct only in movement. It is little to the purpose to maintain that the poets themselves in both languages may remain unconscious of such purposes as we here ascribe to them, that they are merely sensible of having something to say and of saying it by the vehicle that comes nearest to their hand. If this were a fact out of doubt, the accuracy of the analysis would remain undisturbed. What is wholly assured is, that the bias of the Italian mind inclines in the one direction, while the bias of the English mind inclines in the other.

And to a sonnet-thought that is in itself musical, it is but right there should be added a musical setting. Indeed, the one must put the other in motion. What we call the octave shall, therefore, as representing the flow of the wave, bring a slow swell of melody; and the sestet, as representing the ebb, a quicker and shorter beat. Each, doubtless, is best when standing apart as a separate stanza; and each stanza best when compassing an unbroken flood of harmony. In English, however, it is not always possible to achieve so much without injury to the fundamental quality of thought, nor would it always in a series (where variety is an added grace) be desirable even if feasible. Here again we encounter the difficulty which comes of the poverty of our language in rhymes. Beyond question, the use of two rhymes only in the octave is, other things being equal, a perfection to aim after, because it sustains the expectation of the ear at points of the stanza where it would fain (but should not) seek rest. Nevertheless, the use of three rhymes cannot be considered even musically a blemish, for it is matter for doubt if the most sensitive ear is ever conscious of a disturbing influence when the sixth and seventh lines are rhymed separately from the second and third. Indeed, within broad governing limits it may be said to be consistent with the contemporary type of sonnet to adopt whatever rhyme-arrangement may be made to convey a sensible effect as of the forward roll and backward break of a wave of the sea. Only an absolute mastery, however, can be said to warrant any but the least important variation from the metrical structure adopted in the sonnet quoted.

To abandon, in a final word, the impersonal tone of my preface, I may perhaps say I hope I have been able to apply the solvent of a little personal thought to one theory with which we have long been sated. That the English sonnet is a bastard outcome of the Italian has been for no few years the constant imputation. I trust the reproach is in some measure removed.

T. H. C.

Vale of St. John, Cumberland,
1881.

... AUTHORS AND TITLES.

ORIGINAL VERSE. *w first printed.*

BEFORE SUNRISE

ON HELVELLYN.

PAGE

peaks of huge crags uncreate,
he stricken stars usurped demesne,
mutinous vapours to her realm terrene—
comes, the morn inviolate.
th fire, radiant of face, elate,
the lit waves of the steep ravine—
it since eldest time the earth hath seen
e's trail, in heaven articulate.

e world grows old : Behold erelong
the mountains come the swift and strong
le the heights to greet the deathless day ;
abysmal plains the sick and sore
g their feet shall see the imminent gray
has never breathed o'er sea or shore.

T. HALL CAINE.

eademy Jan. 28. 1882

SONNETS

⁂ THE ROMAN NUMERALS AT THE HEADS OF CERTAIN OF THE SONNETS DENOTE THEIR PLACES (AS NUMBERED) IN THE AUTHORS' SEVERAL SERIES.

(1)

HAPPY, ye leaves! whenas those lily hands,
Which hold my life in their dead-doing might,
Shall handle you, and hold in love's soft bands,
Like captives trembling at the victor's sight;
And happy lines! on which, with starry light,
Those lamping eyes will deign sometimes to look,
And read the sorrows of my dying spright,
Written with tears in heart's close-bleeding book;
And happy rhymes! bathed in the sacred brook
Of Helicon, whence she derivèd is;—
When ye behold that Angel's blessèd look,
My soul's long lackèd food, my heaven's bliss,
Leaves, lines and rhymes, seek her to please alone,
Whom if ye please, I care for other none.

(XXXIV)

LIKE as a ship that through the ocean wide
By conduct of some star doth make her way,
Whenas a storm hath dimmed her trusty guide,
Out of her course doth wander far astray,—
So I, whose star, that wont with her bright ray
Me to direct, with clouds is over-cast,
Do wander now in darkness and dismay,
Through hidden perils round about me placed:
Yet hope I well that when this storm is past,
My Helice, the lodestar of my life,
Will shine again and look on me at last,
With lovely light to clear my cloudy grief.
Till then I wander careful, comfortless,
In secret sorrow and sad pensiveness.

(LXVII)

LIKE as a huntsman after weary chase,
Seeing the game from him escaped away,
Sits down to rest him in some shady place,
With panting hounds beguilèd of their prey,—
So, after long pursuit and vain assay,
When I all weary had the chase forsook,
The gentle deer returned the self-same way,
Thinking to quench her thirst at the next brook:
There she, beholding me with milder look,
Sought not to fly, but fearless still did bide;
Till I in hand her yet half trembling took,
And with her own good-will her firmly tied.
Strange thing, me seemed, to see a beast so wild,
So goodly won, with her own will beguiled.

(LXXV)

ONE day I wrote her name upon the strand;
But came the waves and washèd it away:
Again I wrote it with a second hand,
But came the tide and made my pains his prey.
Vain man! said she, that dost in vain assay
A mortal thing so to immortalise;
For I myself shall like to this decay,
And eke my name be wipèd out likewise.
Not so (quoth I); let baser things devise
To die in dust, but you shall live by fame:
My verse your virtues rare shall éternise,
And in the heavens write your glorious name,—
Where, whenas death shall all the world subdue,
Our love shall live, and later life renew.

WITH how sad steps, O Moon, thou climb'st the
skies!
How silently, and with how wan a face!
What, may it be that even in heavenly place
That busy archer his sharp arrows tries?
Sure, if that long-with-love-acquainted eyes
Can judge of love, thou feel'st a lover's case;
I read it in thy looks: thy languished grace,
To me that feel the like, thy state descries.
Then even of fellowship, O Moon, tell me,
Is constant love deemed there but want of wit?
Are beauties there as proud as here they be?
Do they above love to be loved, and yet
Those lovers scorn whom that love doth possess?—
Do they call virtue there ungratefulness?

COME, Sleep, O Sleep! the certain knot of peace,
The baiting-place of wit, the balm of woe,
The poor man's wealth, the prisoner's release,
The indifferent judge between the high and low;
With shield of proof shield me from out the prease
Of those fierce darts Despair at me doth throw;
O make me in these civil wars to cease;
I will good tribute pay, if thou do so.
Take thou of me smooth pillows, sweetest bed,
A chamber deaf of noise and blind of light,
A rosy garland and a weary head:
And if these things, as being thine in right,
Move not thy heavy grace, thou shalt in me,
Livelier than elsewhere, Stella's image see.

SINCE Nature's works be good, and death doth
serve
As Nature's work, why should we fear to die?
Since fear is vain but when it may preserve,
Why should we fear that which we cannot fly?
Fear is more pain than is the pain it fears,
Disarming human minds of native might;
While each conceit an ugly figure bears
Which were not evil, well viewed in reason's light.
Our owly eyes, which dimmed with passions be,
And scarce discern the dawn of coming day,
Let them be clearèd, and begin to see
Our life is but a step in dusty way.
Then let us hold the bliss of peaceful mind;
Since this we feel, great loss we cannot find.

MUSES that sing Love's sensual empery,
And lovers kindling your enragèd fires
At Cupid's bonfires burning in the eye,
Blown with the empty breath of vain desires,—
You that prefer the painted cabinet
Before the wealthy jewels it doth store ye,
That all your joys in dying figures set,
And stain the living substance of your glory;
Abjure those joys, abhor their memory,
And let my Love the honoured subject be
Of love, and honour's complete history;
Your eyes were never yet let in to see
The majesty and riches of the mind,
But dwell in darkness; for your god is blind.

CARE-CHARMER Sleep, son of the sable
Night;
Brother to Death, in silent darkness born;
Relieve my languish, and restore the light;
With dark forgetting of my care return,
And let the day be time enough to mourn
The shipwreck of my ill-adventured youth:
Let waking eyes suffice to wail their scorn,
Without the torment of the Night's untruth.
Cease, dreams, the images of day-desires,
To model forth the passions of the morrow;
Never let rising sun approve you liars,
To add more grief to aggravate my sorrow:
Still let me sleep, embracing clouds in vain,
And never wake to feel the day's disdain.

EAR, why should you command me to my rest,
When now the night doth summon all to sleep?
Methinks this time becometh lovers best:
Night was ordained together friends to keep.
How happy are all other living things,
Which though the day disjoin by several flight,
The quiet Evening yet together brings,
And each returns unto his love at night!
O thou that art so courteous unto all,
Why shouldst thou, Night, abuse me only thus,
That every creature to his kind dost call,
And yet 'tis thou dost only sever us?
Well could I wish it would be ever day,
If, when night comes, you bid me go away.

HOW many paltry, foolish, painted things,
That now in coaches trouble every street,
Shall be forgotten, whom no poet sings,
Ere they be well wrapped in their winding sheet?
Where I to thee eternity shall give
When nothing else remaineth of these days,
And queens hereafter shall be glad to live
Upon the alms of thy superfluous praise;
Virgins and matrons reading these, my rhymes,
Shall be so much delighted with thy story,
That they shall grieve they lived not in these times
To have seen thee their sex's only glory:
So shalt thou fly above the vulgar throng,
Still to survive in my immortal song.

SINCE there's no help, come let us kiss and part,—
Nay I have done, you get no more of me;
And I am glad, yea, glad with all my heart,
That thus so cleanly I myself can free;
Shake hands for ever—cancel all our vows—
And when we meet at any time again,
Be it not seen in either of our brows
That we one jot of former love retain.

Now at the last gasp of Love's latest breath,
When, his pulse failing, Passion speechless lies,
When Faith is kneeling by his bed of death,
And Innocence is closing up his eyes,—
Now if thou would'st, when all have given him over,
From death to life thou might'st him yet recover!

(XXIX)

WHEN in disgrace with fortune and men's eyes,
I all alone beweep my outcast state,
And trouble deaf heaven with my bootless cries,
And look upon myself, and curse my fate,
Wishing me like to one more rich in hope,
Featured like him, like him with friends possessed,
Desiring this man's art, and that man's scope,
With what I most enjoy contented least;
Yet in these thoughts myself almost despising,
Haply I think on thee,—and then my state,
Like to the lark at break of day arising
From sullen earth, sings hymns at heaven's gate;
For thy sweet love remembered such wealth brings,
That then I scorn to change my state with kings.

(XXX)

WHEN to the sessions of sweet silent thought
I summon up remembrance of things past,
I sigh the lack of many a thing I sought,
And with old woes new wail my dear time's waste:
Then can I drown an eye unused to flow,
For precious friends hid in death's dateless night,
And weep afresh love's long-since cancelled woe,
And moan the expense of many a vanished sight:
Then can I grieve at grievances foregone,
And heavily from woe to woe tell o'er
The sad account of fore-bemoanèd moan,
Which I new pay as if not paid before.
But if the while I think on thee, dear friend,
All losses are restored, and sorrows end.

(XXXIII)

FULL many a glorious morning have I seen
Flatter the mountain-tops with sovereign eye,
Kissing with golden face the meadows green,
Gilding pale streams with heavenly alchemy,
Anon permit the basest clouds to ride
With ugly rack on his celestial face,
And from the fórlorn world his visage hide,
Stealing unseen to west with this disgrace:
Even so my sun one early morn did shine
With all triumphant splendour on my brow;
But, out, alack! he was but one hour mine;
The region cloud hath masked him from me now.
Yet him for this my love no whit disdaineth;
Suns of the world may stain when heaven's sun staineth.

(LV)

NOT marble, nor the gilded monuments
Of princes, shall outlive this powerful rhyme;
But you shall shine more bright in these contents
Than unswept stone, besmeared with sluttish time.
When wasteful war shall statues overturn,
And broils root out the work of masonry,
Nor Mars his sword nor war's quick fire shall burn
The living record of your memory.
'Gainst death and all-oblivious enmity
Shall you pace forth; your praise shall still find room,
Even in the eyes of all posterity
That wear this world out to the ending doom.
So till the judgment that yourself arise,
You live in this, and dwell in lovers' eyes.

(LXIV)

WHEN I have seen by Time's fell hand defaced
The rich-proud cost of outworn buried age ;
When sometime lofty towers I see down-razed,
And brass eternal, slave to mortal rage ;
When I have seen the hungry ocean gain
Advantage on the kingdom of the shore,
And the firm soil win of the watery main,
Increasing store with loss, and loss with store ;
When I have seen such interchange of state,
Or state itself confounded to decay ;
Ruin hath taught me thus to ruminate—
That Time will come and take my love away.
This thought is as a death, which cannot choose
But weep to have that which it fears to lose.

(LXVI)

TIRED with all these, for restful death I cry,—
As, to behold desert a beggar born,
And needy nothing trimmed in jollity,
And purest faith unhappily forsworn,
And gilded honour shamefully misplaced,
And maiden virtue rudely strumpeted,
And right perfection wrongfully disgraced,
And strength by limping sway disablèd,
And art made tongue-tied by authority,
And folly (doctor-like) controlling skill,
And simple truth miscalled simplicity,
And captive good attending captain ill:
Tired with all these, from these would I be gone,
Save that, to die, I leave my Love alone.

(LXX)

THAT thou art blamed shall not be thy defect,
For slander's mark was ever yet the fair;
The ornament of beauty is suspect,
A crow that flies in heaven's sweetest air.
So thou be good, slander doth but approve
Thy worth the greater, being wooed of Time;
For canker vice the sweetest buds doth love,
And thou present'st a pure unstainèd prime.
Thou hast passed by the ambush of young days,
Either not assailed, or victor being charged;
Yet this thy praise cannot be so thy praise,
To tie up envy, evermore enlarged:
If some suspect of ill masked not thy show,
Then thou alone kingdoms of hearts shouldst owe.

(LXXI)

NO longer mourn for me when I am dead
Than you shall hear the surly sullen bell
Give warning to the world that I am fled
From this vile world, with vilest worms to dwell :
Nay, if you read this line, remember not
The hand that writ it; for I love you so
That I in your sweet thoughts would be forgot,
If thinking on me then should make you woe.
O, if, I say, you look upon this verse,
When I perhaps compounded am with clay,
Do not so much as my poor name rehearse;
But let your love even with my life decay :
Lest the wise world should look into your moan,
And mock you with me after I am gone.

(LXXIII)

THAT time of year thou mayst in me behold
When yellow leaves, or none, or few, do hang
Upon those boughs which shake against the cold,
Bare ruined choirs where late the sweet birds sang:
In me thou seest the twilight of such day
As after sunset fadeth in the west,
Which by and by black night doth take away,
Death's second self, that seals up all in rest.
In me thou seest the glowing of such fire
That on the ashes of his youth doth lie
As the death-bed whereon it must expire,
Consumed with that which it was nourished by:
This thou perceiv'st, which makes thy love more strong,
To love that well which thou must leave ere long.

(xc)

THEN hate me when thou wilt; if ever, now;
Now, while the world is bent my deeds to cross,
Join with the spite of fortune, make me bow,
And do not drop in for an after-loss:
Ah, do not, when my heart hath 'scaped this sorrow,
Come in the rearward of a conquered woe;
Give not a windy night a rainy morrow,
To linger out a purposed overthrow.
If thou wilt leave me, do not leave me last,
When other petty griefs have done their spite,
But in the onset come; so I shall taste
At first the very worst of fortune's might;
And other strains of woe, which now seem woe,
Compared with loss of thee will not seem so.

(XCIV)

THEY that have power to hurt and will do none,
That do not do the thing they most do show,
Who, moving others, are themselves as stone,
Unmovèd, cold, and to temptation slow,—
They rightly do inherit heaven's graces,
And husband nature's riches from expense;
They are the lords and owners of their faces,
Others but stewards of their excellence.
The summer's flower is to the summer sweet,
Though to itself it only live and die;
But if that flower with base infection meet,
The basest weed out-braves his dignity:
For sweetest things turn sourest by their deeds;
Lilies that fester smell far worse than weeds.

(XCVII)

HOW like a winter hath my absence been
From thee, the pleasure of the fleeting year!
What freezings have I felt, what dark days seen!
What old December's bareness everywhere!
And yet this time removed was summer's time;
The teeming autumn, big with rich increase,
Bearing the wanton burden of the prime,
Like widowed wombs after their lords' decease;
Yet this abundant issue seemed to me
But hope of orphans, and unfathered fruit;
For summer and his pleasures wait on thee,
And, thou away, the very birds are mute;
Or, if they sing, 'tis with so dull a cheer,
That leaves look pale, dreading the winter's near.

(CVII)

NOT mine own fears, nor the prophetic soul
Of the wide world dreaming on things to come
Can yet the lease of my true Love controul,
Supposed as forfeit to a cónfined doom.
The mortal Moon hath her eclipse endured,
And the sad augurs mock their own presage;
Incertainties now crown themselves assured,
And peace proclaims olives of endless age.
Now with the drops of this most balmy time
My love looks fresh, and Death to me subscribes,
Since, spite of him, I 'll live in this poor rhyme,
While he insults o'er dull and speechless tribes:
And thou in this shalt find thy monument,
When tyrants' crests and tombs of brass are spent.

(CXVI)

LET me not to the marriage of true minds
Admit impediments. Love is not love
Which alters when it alteration finds,
Or bends with the remover to remove:
O no! it is an ever-fixèd mark
That looks on tempests and is never shaken;
It is the star to every wandering bark,
Whose worth's unknown, although his height be taken.
Love's not Time's fool, though rosy lips and cheeks
Within his bending sickle's compass come,
Love alters not with his brief hours and weeks,
But bears it out even to the edge of doom.
If this be error, and upon me proved,
I never writ, nor no man ever loved.

(CXXIX)

THE expense of spirit in a waste of shame
Is lust in action ; and till action, lust
Is perjured, murderous, bloody, full of blame,
Savage, extreme, rude, cruel, not to trust ;
Enjoyed no sooner but despisèd straight ;
Past reason hunted ; and no sooner had,
Past reason hated, as a swallow'd bait
On purpose laid to make the taker mad :
Mad in pursuit, and in possession so ;
Had, having, and in quest to have, extreme ;
A bliss in proof, and proved, a very woe ;
Before, a joy proposed ; behind, a dream.
All this the world well knows ; yet none knows well
To shun the heaven that leads men to this hell.

(CXXXVIII)

WHEN my Love swears that she is made of truth
I do believe her, though I know she lies,
That she might think me some untutor'd youth,
Unlearnèd in the world's false subtleties.
Thus vainly thinking that she thinks me young,
Although she knows my days are past the best,
Simply I credit her false-speaking tongue:
On both sides thus is simple truth suppress.
But wherefore says she not she is unjust?
And wherefore say I not that I am old?
O, love's best habit is in seeming trust,
And age in love loves not to have years told;
Therefore I lie with her, and she with me,
And in our faults by lies we flattered be.

(CXLVI)

POOR Soul, the centre of my sinful earth,
Fooled by these rebel powers that thee array,
Why dost thou pine within and suffer dearth,
Painting thy outward walls so costly gay?
Why so large cost, having so short a lease,
Dost thou upon thy fading mansion spend?
Shall worms, inheritors of this excess,
Eat up thy charge? is this thy body's end?
Then, Soul, live thou upon thy servant's loss,
And let that pine to aggravate thy store;
Buy terms divine in selling hours of dross;
Within be fed, without be rich no more:
So shalt thou feed on Death, that feeds on men,
And Death once dead, there's no more dying then!

DEATH, be not proud, though some have callèd thee
Mighty and dreadful, for thou art not so;
For those whom thou think'st thou dost overthrow
Die not, poor Death; nor yet canst thou kill me.
From rest and sleep, which but thy pictures be,
Much pleasure: then from thee, much more must flow;
And soonest our best men do with thee go—
Rest of their bones, and souls' delivery.
Thou 'rt slave to fate, chance, kings, and desperate men,
And dost with poison, war, and sickness dwell,
And poppy or charms can make us sleep as well,
And better than thy stroke. Why swell'st thou then?
One short sleep past, we wake eternally,
And death shall be no more: Death, thou shalt die.

S due by many titles, I resign
Myself to Thee, O God. First I was made
By Thee and for Thee; and, when I was decayed,
Thy blood bought that the which before was Thine;
I am Thy sun, made with Thyself to shine,
Thy servant whose pains Thou hast still repaid,
Thy sheep, Thine image, and, till I betrayed
Myself, a temple of Thy Spirit divine.
Why doth the devil then usurp on me?
Why doth he steal, nay, ravish that 's Thy right?
Except Thou rise, and for Thine own work fight,
Oh! I shall soon despair, when I do see
That Thou lov'st mankind well, yet wilt not choose me,
And Satan hates me, yet is loth to lose me.

AT the round earth's imagined corners blow
Your trumpets, angels, and arise, arise
From death, you numberless infinities
Of souls, and to your scattered bodies go,
All whom the Flood did, and Fire shall, o'erthrow;
All whom DEATH, war, age, agues, tyrannies,
Despair, law, chance hath slain; and you whose eyes
Shall behold God, and never taste death's woe;
But let them sleep, Lord, and me mourn a space;
For if above all those my sins abound,
'Tis late to ask abundance of Thy grace,
When we are there. Here on this lowly ground
Teach me how to repent; for that 's as good
As if Thou 'dst sealed my pardon with my blood.

TO SLEEP.

SLEEP, Silence' child, sweet father of soft rest,
Prince whose approach peace to all mortals brings,
Indifferent host to shepherds and to kings,
Sole comforter of minds which are oppressed;
Lo! by thy charming-rod all breathing things
Lie slumbering, with forgetfulness possessed,
And yet o'er me to spread thy drowsy wings
Thou spar'st alas! who cannot be thy guest.
Since I am thine, O come, but with that face
To inward light which thou art wont to show;
With feignèd solace ease a true-felt woe;
Or if, deaf god, thou do deny that grace,
Come as thou wilt, and what thou wilt bequeath;
I long to kiss the image of my death.

THE GOLDEN AGE.

WHAT hapless hap had I for to be born
In these unhappy times, and dying days
Of this now doting world, when good decays,
Love's quite extinct, and virtue's held a scorn?
When such are only prized by wretched ways
Who with a golden fleece them can adorn;
When avarice and lust are counted praise,
And bravest minds live, orphan-like, forlorn!
Why was not I born in that golden age
When gold was not yet known?—and those black arts
By which base worldlings vilely play their parts,
With horrid acts staining earth's stately stage?
To have been then, O heaven! 't had been my bliss,
But bless me now, and take me soon from this.

THE BOOK OF THE WORLD.

OF this fair volume which we World do name
If we the sheets and leaves could turn with care,
Of him who it corrects and did it frame
We clear might read the art and wisdom rare:
Find out his power which wildest powers doth tame,
His providence extending everywhere,
His justice which proud rebels doth not spare,
In every page, no, period of the same.
But silly we, like foolish children, rest
Well pleased with coloured vellum, leaves of gold,
Fair dangling ribands, leaving what is best,—
On the great writer's sense ne'er taking hold;
Or if by chance our minds do muse on ought,
It is some picture on the margin wrought.

IF crost with all mishaps be my poor life,
If one short day I never spent in mirth,
If my spright with itself holds lasting strife,
If sorrow's death is but new sorrow's birth;
If this vain world be but a sable stage
Where slave-born man plays to the scoffing stars;
If youth be tossed with love, with weakness age,
If knowledge serve to hold our thoughts in wars;
If time can close the hundred mouths of fame,
And make what long since passed like that to be;
If virtue only be an idle name;
If I when I was born was born to die,—
Why seek I to prolong these loathsome days?
The fairest rose in shortest time decays.

AH! burning thoughts, now let me take some rest,
And your tumultuous broils awhile appease;
Is 't not enough, stars, fortune, love molest
Me all at once, but ye must too displease?
Let hope, though false, yet lodge within my breast;
My high attempt, though dangerous, yet praise.
What though I trace not right heaven's steepy ways?
It doth suffice my fall shall make me blest.
I do not doat on days, nor fear not death:
So that my life be brave, what though not long?
Let me renowned live from the vulgar throng,
And when ye list, Heavens! take this borrowed breath.
Men but like visions are, Time all doth claim:
He lives who dies to win a lasting name.

AIREST, when by the rules of palmistry
You took my hand to try if you could guess,
By lines therein, if any wight there be
Ordained to make me know some happiness,
I wished that those charácters could explain
Whom I will never wrong with hope to win;
Or that by them a copy might be seen
By you, O Love, what thoughts I have within.
But since the hand of Nature did not set
(As providently loth to have it known)
The means to find that hidden alphabet,
Mine eyes shall be the interpreters alone.
By them conceive my thoughts and tell me fair,
If now you see her that doth love me there!

SIN.

LORD, with what care hast Thou begirt us round!
Parents first season us; then schoolmasters
Deliver us to laws; they send us bound
To rules of reason, holy messengers,
Pulpits and Sundays, sorrow dogging sin,
Afflictions sorted, anguish of all sizes,
Fine nets and stratagems to catch us in,
Bibles laid open, millions of surprises,
Blessings beforehand, ties of gratefulness,
The sound of glory ringing in our ears;
Without, our shame; within, our consciences:
Angels and grace, eternal hopes and fears.
Yet all these fences and their whole array
One cunning bosom-sin blows quite away.

LADY, that in the prime of earliest youth
 Wisely hast shunned the broad way and the
  green,
 And with those few art eminently seen
That labour up the hill of heavenly truth,
The better part with Mary and with Ruth
 Chosen thou hast; and they that overween,
 And at thy growing virtues fret their spleen,
No anger find in thee, but pity and ruth.
Thy care is fixed, and zealously attends
 To fill thy odorous lamp with deeds of light,
  And hope that reaps not shame. Therefore be sure
Thou, when the Bridegroom with his feastful friends
 Passes to bliss at the mid-hour of night,
  Hast gained thy entrance, Virgin wise and pure.

TO THE LORD GENERAL CROMWELL.

CROMWELL, our chief of men, who through a cloud
Not of war only, but detractions rude,
Guided by faith and matchless fortitude,
To peace and truth thy glorious way hast ploughed,
And on the neck of crowned fortune proud
Hast reared God's trophies, and his work pursued,
While Darwen stream, with blood of Scots imbrued,
And Dunbar field resounds thy praises loud,
And Worcester's laureate wreath: Yet much remains
To conquer still; Peace hath her victories
No less renowned than War: new foes arise,
Threatening to bind our souls with secular chains:—
Help us to save free conscience from the paw
Of hireling wolves, whose gospel is their maw.

TO SIR HENRY VANE THE YOUNGER.

VANE, young in years, but in sage counsel old,
Than whom a better senator ne'er held
The helm of Rome, when gowns, not arms, repelled
The fierce Epirot, and the African bold,
Whether to settle peace, or to unfold
The drift of hollow states hard to be spelled;
Then to advise how War may best, upheld,
Move by her two main nerves, iron and gold,
In all her equipage; besides to know
Both spiritual power and civil, what each means,
What severs each, thou hast learned, which few have done:
The bounds of either sword to thee we owe:
Therefore on thy firm hand Religion leans
In peace, and reckons thee her eldest son.

ON THE LATE MASSACRE IN PIEDMONT.

AVENGE, O Lord, thy slaughtered saints, whose bones
Lie scattered on the Alpine mountains cold;
Even them who kept thy truth so pure of old,
When all our fathers worshipped stocks and stones,
Forget not; in thy book record their groans
Who were thy sheep, and in their ancient fold
Slain by the bloody Piemontese, that rolled
Mother with infant down the rocks. Their moans
The vales redoubled to the hills, and they
To Heaven. Their martyred blood and ashes sow
O'er all the Italian fields, where still doth sway
The triple Tyrant; that from these may grow
A hundred-fold, who having learnt thy way,
Early may fly the Babylonian woe.

METHOUGHT I saw my late espousèd saint
Brought to me like Alcestis from the grave,
Whom Jove's great son to her glad husband gave,
Rescued from Death by force, though pale and faint.
Mine, as whom washed from spot of child-bed taint
Purification in the Old Law did save,
And such, as yet once more I trust to have
Full sight of her in Heaven without restraint,
Came vested all in white, pure as her mind:
Her face was veiled, yet to my fancied sight
Love, sweetness, goodness, in her person shined
So clear, as in no face with more delight.
But O, as to embrace me she inclined,
I waked, she fled, and day brought back my night.

WHEN I consider how my light is spent
Ere half my days in this dark world and wide,
And that one talent, which is death to hide,
Lodged with me useless, though my soul more bent
To serve therewith my Maker, and present
My true account, lest He, returning, chide;
'Doth God exact day-labour, light denied?'
I fondly ask: But Patience, to prevent
That murmur, soon replies: 'God doth not need
Either man's work, or his own gifts. Who best
Bear his mild yoke, they serve him best. His state
Is kingly: thousands at his bidding speed
And post o'er land and ocean without rest;
They also serve who only stand and wait.'

CYRIACK, this three-years-day these eyes, though clear,
To outward view, of blemish or of spot,
Bereft of light, their seeing have forgot;
Nor to their idle orbs doth sight appear
Of sun, or moon, or star, throughout the year,
Or man, or woman. Yet I argue not
Against Heaven's hand or will, nor bate a jot
Of heart or hope, but still bear up and steer
Right onward. What supports me, dost thou ask?
The conscience, friend, to have lost them overplied
In Liberty's defence, my noble task,
Of which all Europe rings from side to side.
This thought might lead me through the world's vain mask,
Content though blind, had I no better guide.

TO WILLIAMSON.

WHEN I behold thee, blameless Williamson,
Wrecked like an infant on a savage shore,
While others round on borrowed pinions soar,
My busy fancy calls thy thread mis-spun;
Till Faith instructs me the deceit to shun,
While thus she speaks: 'Those wings that from the store
Of virtue were not lent, howe'er they bore
In this gross air, will melt when near the sun.
The truly ambitious wait for Nature's time,
Content by certain though by slow degrees
To mount above the reach of vulgar flight;
Nor is that man confined to this low clime
Who but the extremest skirts of glory sees,
And hears celestial echoes with delight.'

ON THE DEATH OF RICHARD WEST.

IN vain to me the smiling mornings shine,
And reddening Phœbus lifts his golden fire;
The birds in vain their amorous descant join;
Or cheerful fields resume their green attire:
These ears, alas! for other notes repine,
A different object do these eyes require;
My lonely anguish melts no heart but mine,
And in my breast the imperfect joys expire.
Yet morning smiles the busy race to cheer,
And newborn pleasure brings to happier men;
The fields to all their wonted tribute bear;
To warm their little loves the birds complain;
I fruitless mourn to him that cannot hear,
And weep the more because I weep in vain.

TO MARY UNWIN.

MARY! I want a lyre with other strings,
Such aid from heaven as some have feigned they drew,
An eloquence scarce given to mortals, new
And undebased by praise of meaner things;
That, ere through age or woe I shed my wings,
I may record thy worth with honour due,
In verse as musical as thou art true,
And that immortalizes whom it sings.
But thou hast little need. There is a Book
By seraphs writ with beams of heavenly light,
On which the eyes of God not rarely look,
A chronicle of actions just and bright;—
There all thy deeds, my faithful Mary, shine;
And since thou own'st that praise, I spare thee mine.

DECEMBER MORNING.

LOVE to rise ere gleams the tardy light,
Winter's pale dawn; and as warm fires illume,
And cheerful tapers shine around the room,
Through misty windows bend my musing sight,
Where, round the dusky lawn, the mansions white,
With shutters closed, peer faintly through the gloom
That slow recedes; while yon grey spires assume,
Rising from their dark pile, an added height
By indistinctness given.—Then to decree
The grateful thoughts to God, ere they unfold
To friendship or the Muse, or seize with glee
Wisdom's rich page. O hours more worth than gold,
By whose blest use we lengthen life, and, free
From drear decays of age, outlive the old!

TO HOPE.

EVER skilled to wear the form we love!
To bid the shapes of fear and grief depart;
Come, gentle Hope! with one gay smile remove
The lasting sadness of an aching heart.
Thy voice, benign enchantress! let me hear;
Say that for me some pleasures yet shall bloom,—
That fancy's radiance, friendship's precious tear,
Shall soften, or shall chase, misfortune's gloom.
But come not glowing in the dazzling ray
Which once with dear illusions charmed my eye;
O, strew no more, sweet flatterer! on my way
The flowers I fondly thought too bright to die:
Visions less fair will soothe my pensive breast,
That asks not happiness, but longs for rest.

ON ECHO AND SILENCE.

IN eddying course when leaves began to fly,
And Autumn in her lap the store to strew,
As 'mid wild scenes I chanced the Muse to woo,
Through glens untrod and woods that frowned on high,
Two sleeping nymphs with wonder mute I spy!—
And lo, she 's gone!—in robe of dark green hue,
'Twas Echo from her sister Silence flew:
For quick the hunter's horn resounded to the sky!
In shade affrighted Silence melts away.
Not so her sister!—hark, for onward still
With far-heard step she takes her listening way,
Bounding from rock to rock, and hill to hill!
Ah, mark the merry maid in mockful play
With thousand mimic tones the laughing forest fill.

TIME! who know'st a lenient hand to lay
Softest on sorrow's wound, and slowly thence,
Lulling to sad repose the weary sense,
The faint pang stealest unperceived away;
On thee I rest my only hope at last,
And think, when thou hast dried the bitter tear
That flows in vain o'er all my soul held dear,
I may look back on every sorrow past,
And meet life's peaceful evening with a smile;—
As some lone bird, at day's departing hour,
Sings in the sunbeam, of the transient shower
Forgetful, though its wings are wet the while:—
Yet ah! how much must that poor heart endure,
Which hopes from thee, and thee alone, a cure!

LEMNOS.

ON this lone isle, whose rugged rocks affright
The cautious pilot, ten revolving years
Great Pæan's son, unwonted erst to tears,
Wept o'er his wound ; alike each rolling light
Of heaven he watched, and blamed its lingering flight ;
By day the sea-mew screaming round his cave
Drove slumber from his eyes ; the chiding wave
And savage howlings chased his dreams by night.
Hope still was his : in each low breeze that sighed
Through his low grot he heard a coming oar—
In each white cloud a coming sail he spied ;
Nor seldom listened to the fancied roar
Of Oeta's torrents, or the hoarser tide
That parts famed Trachis from the Euboic shore.

THE SONNET.

UNS fret not at their convent's narrow room ;
And hermits are contented with their cells ;
And students with their pensive citadels ;
Maids at the wheel, the weaver at his loom,
Sit blithe and happy ; bees that soar for bloom
High as the highest peak of Furness fells
Will murmur by the hour in foxglove bells :
In truth, the prison unto which we doom
Ourselves no prison is ; and hence to me
In sundry moods 'twas pastime to be bound
Within the Sonnet's scanty plot of ground :
Pleased if some souls (for such there needs must be)
Who have felt the weight of too much liberty,
Should find brief solace there, as I have found.

COMPOSED UPON WESTMINSTER BRIDGE IN EARLY MORNING, SEPTEMBER 3, 1802.

EARTH has not anything to show more fair:
Dull would he be of soul who could pass by
A sight so touching in its majesty:
This city now doth like a garment wear
The beauty of the morning; silent, bare,
Ships, towers, domes, theatres, and temples lie
Open unto the fields and to the sky;
All bright and glittering in the smokeless air.
Never did sun more beautifully steep
In his first splendour valley, rock, or hill;
Ne'er saw I, never felt, a calm so deep!
The river glideth at his own sweet will:
Dear God! the very houses seem asleep;
And all that mighty heart is lying still!

IT is a beauteous Evening, calm and free;
The holy time is quiet as a Nun
Breathless with adoration; the broad sun
Is sinking down in its tranquillity;
The gentleness of heaven is on the Sea:
Listen! the mighty Being is awake,
And doth with his eternal motion make
A sound like thunder—everlastingly.

Dear Child! dear Girl! that walkest with me here,
If thou appear untouched by solemn thought,
Thy nature therefore is not less divine:
Thou liest 'in Abraham's bosom' all the year;
And worshipp'st at the Temple's inner shrine,
God being with thee when we know it not.

IT is not to be thought of that the Flood
Of British freedom, which, to the open sea
Of the world's praise, from dark antiquity
Hath flowed, 'with pomp of waters, unwithstood'—
Roused though it be full often to a mood
Which spurns the check of salutary bands,—
That this most famous Stream in bogs and sands
Should perish; and to evil and to good
Be lost for ever. In our halls is hung
Armoury of the invincible Knights of old:
We must be free or die, who speak the tongue
That Shakspeare spake—the faith and morals hold
Which Milton held. In everything we 're sprung
Of Earth's first blood, have titles manifold.

MILTON! thou shouldst be living at this hour:
England hath need of thee: she is a fen
Of stagnant waters: altar, sword, and pen,
Fireside, the heroic wealth of hall and bower,
Have forfeited their ancient English dower
Of inward happiness. We are selfish men;
Oh! raise us up, return to us again;
And give us manners, virtue, freedom, power.
Thy soul was like a star, and dwelt apart:
Thou hadst a voice whose sound was like the sea:
Pure as the naked heavens, majestic, free,
So didst thou travel on life's common way
In cheerful godliness; and yet thy heart
The lowliest duties on herself did lay.

WHEN I have borne in memory what has tamed
Great Nations, how ennobling thoughts depart
When men change swords for ledgers, and desert
The student's bower for gold, some fears unnamed
I had, my Country!—am I to be blamed?
Now, when I think of thee, and what thou art,
Verily, in the bottom of my heart,
Of those unfilial fears I am ashamed.
For dearly must we prize thee; we who find
In thee a bulwark for the cause of men;
And I by my affection was beguiled:
What wonder if a Poet now and then,
Among the many movements of his mind,
Felt for thee as a lover or a child.

THE world is too much with us; late and soon,
  Getting and spending, we lay waste our powers:
  Little we see in Nature that is ours;
We have given our hearts away, a sordid boon!
This sea that bares her bosom to the moon,
  The winds that will be howling at all hours
  And are up-gathered now like sleeping flowers;
For this, for every thing, we are out of tune;
It moves us not.—Great God! I 'd rather be
  A pagan suckled in a creed outworn;
So might I, standing on this pleasant lea,
  Have glimpses that would make me less forlorn;
Have sight of Proteus rising from the sea;
  Or hear old Triton blow his wreathèd horn.

ON THE EXTINCTION OF THE VENETIAN REPUBLIC.

NCE did She hold the gorgeous East in fee,
And was the safeguard of the West: the worth
Of Venice did not fall below her birth—
Venice, the eldest Child of Liberty!
She was a maiden City, bright and free;
No guile seduced, no force could violate;
And when she took unto herself a Mate,
She must espouse the everlasting Sea.

And what if she has seen these glories fade,
Those titles vanish, and that strength decay;
Yet shall some tribute of regret be paid
When her long life hath reached its final day;
Men are we, and must grieve when even the shade
Of that which once was great is passed away.

TO TOUSSAINT L'OUVERTURE.

TOUSSAINT, the most unhappy man of men!
Whether the all-cheering sun be free to shed
His beams around thee, or thou rest thy head
Pillowed in some dark dungeon's earless den:—
O miserable Chieftain! where and when
Wilt thou find patience? Yet die not; do thou
Wear rather in thy bonds a cheerful brow:
Though fallen thyself, never to rise again,
Live, and take comfort. Thou hast left behind
Powers that will work for thee: air, earth and skies;
There's not a breathing of the common wind
That will forget thee; thou hast great allies;
Thy friends are exultations, agonies,
And love, and man's unconquerable mind.

MARY QUEEN OF SCOTS LANDING AT THE MOUTH OF THE DERWENT.

DEAR to the Loves, and to the Graces vowed,
The Queen drew back the wimple that she wore;
And to the throng, that on the Cumbrian shore
Her landing hailed, how touchingly she bowed;
And like a Star (that, from a heavy cloud
Of pine-tree foliage poised in air, forth darts,
When a soft summer gale at evening parts
The gloom that did its loveliness enshroud)
She smiled; but time, the old Saturnian seer,
Sighed on the wing as her foot pressed the strand,
With step prolusive to a long array
Of woes and degradations hand in hand—
Weeping captivity, and shuddering fear
Stilled by the ensanguined block of Fotheringay!

THE RIVER DUDDON.

WHAT aspect bore the Man who roved or fled,
First of his tribe, to this dark dell—who first
In this pellucid Current slaked his thirst?
What hopes came with him? what designs were spread
Along his path? His unprotected bed
What dreams encompassed? Was the intruder nursed
In hideous usages, and rites accursed,
That thinned the living and disturbed the dead?
No voice replies;—both air and earth are mute;
And thou, blue Streamlet, murmuring yield'st no more
Than a soft record, that, whatever fruit
Of ignorance thou might'st witness heretofore,
Thy function was to heal and to restore,
To soothe and cleanse, not madden and pollute.

OH it is pleasant, with a heart at ease,
Just after sunset, or by moonlight skies,
To make the shifting clouds be what you please,
Or let the easily-persuaded eyes
Own each quaint likeness issuing from the mould
Of a friend's fancy; or, with head bent low
And cheek aslant, see rivers flow of gold
'Twixt crimson banks; and then, a traveller, go
From mount to mount through Cloudland, gorgeous land!
Or listening to the tide, with closèd sight,
Be that blind bard who, on the Chian strand
By those deep sounds possessed with inward light,
Beheld the Iliad and the Odyssee
Rise to the swelling of the voiceful sea.

ON A RUINED HOUSE IN A ROMANTIC COUNTRY.

ND this reft house is that, the which he built,
Lamented Jack! and here his malt he piled,
Cautious in vain! these rats that squeak so wild,
Squeak not unconscious of their father's guilt.
Did he not see her gleaming through the glade?
Belike 'twas she, the maiden all forlorn.
What though she milked no cow with crumpled horn,
Yet, aye she haunts the dale where erst she strayed:
And, aye beside her stalks her amorous knight!
Still on his thighs their wonted brogues are worn,
And through those brogues, still tattered and betorn,
His hindward charms gleam an unearthly white.
Ah! thus through broken clouds at night's high noon
Peeps in fair fragments forth the full-orb'd harvest moon!

WINTER.

WRINKLED, crabbèd man they picture thee,
Old Winter, with a rugged beard as grey
As the long moss upon the apple-tree;
Blue-lipt, an icedrop at thy sharp blue nose,
Close muffled up, and on thy dreary way
Plodding alone through sleet and drifting snows.
They should have drawn thee by the high-heapt hearth,
Old Winter! seated in thy great armed chair,
Watching the children at their Christmas mirth;
Or circled by them as thy lips declare
Some merry jest, or tale of murder dire,
Or troubled spirit that disturbs the night,
Pausing at times to rouse the mouldering fire,
Or taste the old October brown and bright.

WORK.

WHO first invented Work, and bound the free
And holyday-rejoicing spirit down
To the ever-haunting importunity
Of business in the green fields, and the town—
To plough, loom, anvil, spade—and oh! most sad,
To that dry drudgery at the desk's dead wood?
Who but the Being unblest, alien from good,
Sabbathless Satan! he who his unglad
Task ever plies 'mid rotatory burnings,
That round and round incalculably reel—
For wrath divine hath made him like a wheel—
In that red realm from which are no returnings:
Where toiling, and turmoiling, ever and aye,
He, and his thoughts, keep pensive working-day.

TIMID grace sits trembling in her eye,
  As loth to meet the rudeness of men's sight,
  Yet shedding a delicious lunar light
That steeps in kind oblivious ecstasy
The care-crazed mind, like some still melody:
  Speaking most plain the thoughts which do possess
  Her gentle sprite: peace, and meek quietness,
And innocent loves, and maiden purity:
A look whereof might heal the cruel smart
  Of changed friends, or fortune's wrongs unkind:
Might to sweet deeds of mercy move the heart
  Of him who hates his brethren of mankind.
Turned are those lights from me, who fondly yet
Past joys, vain loves, and buried hopes regret.

TO NIGHT.

MYSTERIOUS Night! when our first parent knew
Thee from report divine, and heard thy name,
Did he not tremble for this lovely frame,
This glorious canopy of light and blue?
Yet 'neath a curtain of translucent dew,
Bathed in the rays of the great setting flame,
Hesperus with the host of heaven came,
And lo! Creation widened in man's view.

Who could have thought such darkness lay concealed
Within thy beams, O Sun! or who could find,
Whilst fly and leaf and insect stood revealed,
That to such countless orbs thou mad'st us blind!
Why do we then shun Death with anxious strife?
If Light can thus deceive, wherefore not Life?

ON HEARING MYSELF FOR THE FIRST TIME CALLED AN OLD MAN ÆT. 50.

AGES have rolled within my breast, though yet
  Not nigh the bourn to fleeting man assigned:
  Yes: old—alas how spent the struggling mind
Which at the noon of life is fain to set!
My dawn and evening have so closely met
  That men the shades of night begin to find
  Darkening my brow; and heedless, not unkind,
Let the sad warning drop, without regret.

Gone Youth! had I thus missed thee, nor a hope
  Were left of thy return beyond the tomb,
I could curse life:—But glorious is the scope
  Of an immortal soul.—Oh Death, thy gloom
Short, and already tinged with coming light,
Is to the Christian but a Summer's night.

FOUNTAINS ABBEY.

ABBEY! for ever smiling pensively,
How like a thing of Nature thou dost rise
Amid her loveliest works! as if the skies,
Clouded with grief, were arched thy roof to be,
And the tall trees were copied all from thee!
Mourning thy fortunes—while the waters dim
Flow like the memory of thy evening hymn,
Beautiful in their sorrowing sympathy;
As if they with a weeping sister wept,
Winds name thy name! But thou, though sad, art calm,
And Time with thee his plighted troth hath kept;
For harebells deck thy brow, and, at thy feet,
Where sleep the proud, the bee and redbreast meet,
Mixing thy sighs with Nature's lonely psalm.

TO THE HARVEST MOON.

AGAIN thou reignest in thy golden hall,
Rejoicing in thy sway, fair queen of night!
The ruddy reapers hail thee with delight:
Theirs is the harvest, theirs the joyous call
For tasks well ended ere the season's fall.
Sweet orb, thou smilest from thy starry height;
But whilst on them thy beams are shedding bright,
To me thou com'st o'ershadowed with a pall:
To me alone the year hath fruitless flown;
Earth hath fulfilled her trust through all her lands,
The good man gathereth now where he had sown,
And the Great Master in his vineyard stands;
But I, as if my task were all unknown,
Come to his gates alas! with empty hands.

TO THE GRASSHOPPER AND THE CRICKET.

GREEN little vaulter in the sunny grass,
Catching your heart up at the feel of June,
Sole voice that 's heard amidst the lazy noon,
When even the bees lag at the summoning brass;
And you, warm little housekeeper, who class
With those who think the candles come too soon,
Loving the fire, and with your tricksome tune
Nick the glad silent moments as they pass;
Oh sweet and tiny cousins, that belong
One to the fields, the other to the hearth,
Both have your sunshine; both, though small, are strong
At your clear hearts; and both were sent on earth
To sing in thoughtful ears this natural song:
In-doors and out, summer and winter,—Mirth.

THE NILE.

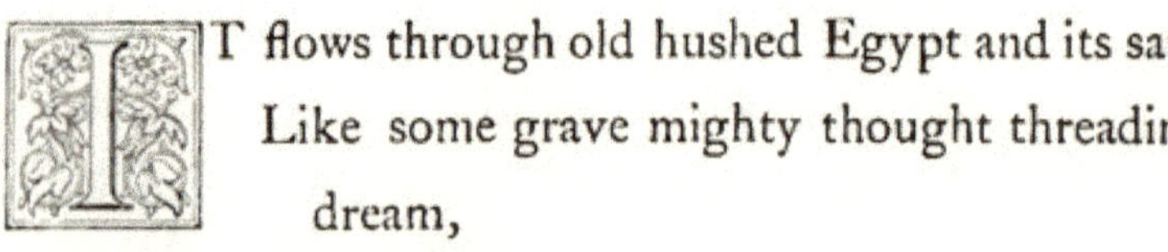

IT flows through old hushed Egypt and its sands,
  Like some grave mighty thought threading a dream,
  And times and things, as in that vision, seem
Keeping along it their eternal stands,—
Caves, pillars, pyramids, the shepherd bands
  That roamed through the young world, the glory extreme
  Of high Sesostris, and that southern beam,
The laughing queen that caught the world's great hands.

  Then comes a mightier silence, stern and strong,
  As of a world left empty of its throng,
And the void weighs on us; and then we wake,
  And hear the fruitful stream lapsing along
'Twixt villages, and think how we shall take
Our own calm journey on for human sake.

WHAT art Thou, Mighty One, and where Thy seat?
Thou broodest on the calm that cheers the lands,
And Thou dost bear within Thine awful hands
The rolling thunders and the lightnings fleet;
Stern on Thy dark-wrought car of cloud and wind
Thou guid'st the northern storm at night's dead noon,
Or on the red wing of the fierce monsoon
Disturb'st the sleeping giant of the Ind.
In the drear silence of the polar span
Dost Thou repose? or in the solitude
Of sultry tracts, where the lone caravan
Hears nightly howl the tiger's hungry brood?
Vain thought, the confines of His throne to trace
Who glows through all the fields of boundless space!

IS this the spot where Rome's eternal foe
Into his snares the mighty legions drew,
Whence from the carnage, spiritless and few,
A remnant scarcely reached her gates of woe?
Is this the stream, thus gliding soft and slow,
That, from the gushing wounds of thousands, grew
So fierce a flood, that waves of crimson hue
Rushed on the bosom of the lake below?
The mountains that gave back the battle-cry
Are silent now; perchance yon hillocks green
Mark where the bones of those old warriors lie.
Heaven never gladdened a more peaceful scene;
Never left softer breeze a fairer sky
To sport upon thy waters, Thrasymene!

THE ROCK OF CASHEL.

ROYAL and saintly Cashel! I would gaze
Upon the wreck of thy departed powers
Not in the dewy light of matin hours,
Nor the meridian pomp of summer's blaze,
But at the close of dim autumnal days,
When the sun's parting glance, through slanting showers,
Sheds o'er thy rock-throned battlements and towers
Such awful gleams as brighten o'er Decay's
Prophetic cheek. At such a time, methinks,
There breathes from thy lone courts and voiceless aisles
A melancholy moral; such as sinks
On the lone traveller's heart, amid the piles
Of vast Persepolis on her mountain stand,
Or Thebes half buried in the desert sand.

THE MAN OF GLENCOE.

IF this be true, that from thy lip, or hand,
The mandate passed—or the inexpressive eye
Kindling to keen, yet cold ferocity,
Consented—or that hints forestalled command—
Too long hath Vengeance slept: too long the brand
Of shame by flattering wreaths been hid. To die
Untimely, yet unjudged, doth not imply
Atonement. Rise, at last, and take thy stand,
Great King! before the Avenger! Wake—arise!
Posterity, the Judge, amid the cries
Of the unforgotten slain, his sentence slow
Records;—for desecrated household ties?—
For wrong fraternal? filial treason?—No!
Grave on his tomb but one dark word: 'Glencoe.'

CHILLON.

ETERNAL Spirit of the chainless Mind!
Brightest in dungeons, Liberty, thou art;—
For there thy habitation is the heart,—
The heart which love of thee alone can bind;
And when thy sons to fetters are consigned,
To fetters, and the damp vault's dayless gloom,
Their country conquers with their martyrdom,
And Freedom's fame finds wings on every wind.

Chillon! thy prison is a holy place,
And thy sad floor an altar, for 'twas trod,
Until his very steps have left a trace,
Worn, as if thy cold pavement were a sod,
By Bonnivard! May none those marks efface!
For they appeal from tyranny to God.

ANGLING.

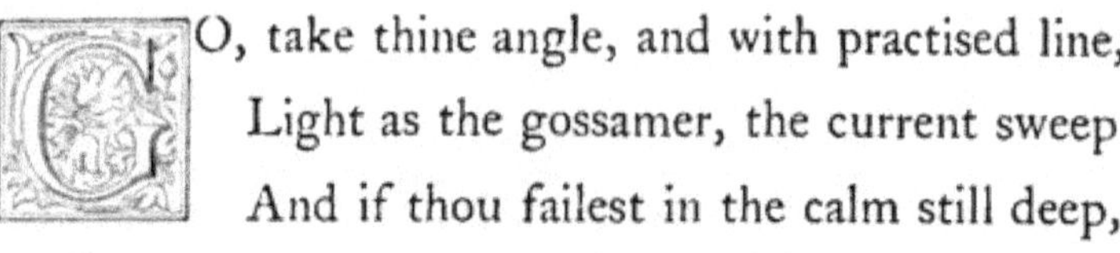

O, take thine angle, and with practised line,
Light as the gossamer, the current sweep;
And if thou failest in the calm still deep,
In the rough eddy may a prize be thine.
Say thou'rt unlucky where the sunbeams shine;
Beneath the shadow, where the waters creep,
Perchance the monarch of the brook shall leap—
For fate is ever better than design.
Still persevere; the giddiest breeze that blows,
For thee may blow, with fame and fortune rife;
Be prosperous—and what reck if it arose
Out of some pebble with the stream at strife,
Or that the light wind dallied with the boughs?
Thou art successful;—such is human life.

THE SEA—IN CALM.

LOOK what immortal floods the sunset pours
Upon us!—Mark how still (as though in dreams
Bound) the once wild and terrible Ocean seems!
How silent are the winds! No billow roars,
But all is tranquil as Elysian shores;
The silver margin which aye runneth round
The moon-enchanted sea hath here no sound:
Even Echo speaks not on these radiant moors.
What! is the giant of the ocean dead,
Whose strength was all unmatched beneath the sun?
No: he reposes. Now his toils are done,
More quiet than the babbling brooks is he.
So mightiest powers by deepest calms are fed,
And sleep, how oft, in things that gentlest be.

YE hasten to the grave! what seek ye there,
Ye restless thoughts and busy purposes
Of the idle brain, which the world's livery wear?
O thou quick heart, which pantest to possess
All that anticipation feigneth fair!
Thou vainly curious mind, which wouldest guess
Whence thou didst come, and whither thou may'st go,
And that which never yet was known wouldst know—
O, whither hasten ye, that thus ye press
With such swift feet life's green and pleasant path,
Seeking alike from happiness and woe
A refuge in the cavern of grey death?
O heart, and mind, and thoughts! what thing do you
Hope to inherit in the grave below?

OZYMANDIAS.

MET a traveller from an antique land
Who said: Two vast and trunkless legs of stone
Stand in the desert. Near them, on the sand,
Half sunk, a shattered visage lies, whose frown
And wrinkled lip and sneer of cold command
Tell that its sculptor well those passions read
Which yet survive, stamped on these lifeless things,
The hand that mocked them and the heart that fed;
And on the pedestal these words appear:
'My name is Ozymandias, King of Kings:
Look on my works, ye Mighty, and despair!'
Nothing beside remains. Round the decay
Of that colossal wreck, boundless and bare
The lone and level sands stretch far away.

TO THE MEMORY OF SAMUEL MARTIN,

MY VENERABLE GRANDFATHER-IN-LAW, WHO WAS TAKEN AWAY FROM US IN THE NINETIETH YEAR OF HIS LIFE, AND THE SIXTY-EIGHTH OF HIS MINISTRY.

FAREWELL on man's dark journey o'er the deep,
Thou sire of sires! whose bow in strength hath stood
These threescore years and ten that thou hast wooed
Men's souls to heaven. In Jesus fallen asleep,
Around thy couch three generations weep,
Reared on thy knees with wisdom's heavenly food,
And by thy counsels taught to choose the good;
Who in thy footsteps press up Zion's steep,
To reach that temple which but now did ope
And let their father in. O'er *his* bier wake
No doleful strain, but high the note of hope
And praise uplift to God, who did him make
A faithful shepherd, of his Church a prop;
And of his seed did faithful shepherds take.

SPRING FLOWERS.

THE loveliest flowers the closest cling to earth,
And they first feel the sun: so violets blue:
So the soft star-like primrose drenched in dew
The happiest of Spring's happy fragrant birth.
To gentlest touches sweetest tones reply.
Still humbleness with her low-breathèd voice
Can steal o'er man's proud heart, and win his choice
From earth to heaven, with mightier witchery
Than eloquence or wisdom e'er could own.
Bloom on then in your shade, contented bloom,
Sweet flowers, nor deem yourselves to all unknown,—
Heaven knows you, by whose gales and dews ye thrive;
They know, who one day for their altered doom
Shall thank you, taught by you to abase themselves and live.

FIRST SIGHT OF SPRING.

THE hazel-blooms, in threads of crimson hue,
Peep through the swelling buds, foretelling Spring,
Ere yet a white-thorn leaf appears in view,
Or March finds throstles pleased enough to sing.
To the old touchwood tree woodpeckers cling
A moment, and their harsh-toned notes renew;
In happier mood, the stockdove claps his wing;
The squirrel sputters up the powdered oak,
With tail cocked o'er his head, and ears erect,
Startled to hear the woodman's understroke;
And with the courage that his fears collect,
He hisses fierce, half malice and half glee,
Leaping from branch to branch about the tree,
In winter's foliage, moss and lichens, deckt.

THE HAPPY BIRD.

THE happy white-throat on the swaying bough,
Rocked by the impulse of the gadding wind
That ushers in the showers of April, now
Carols right joyously ; and now reclined,
Crouching, she clings close to her moving seat,
To keep her hold ;—and till the wind for rest
Pauses, she mutters inward melodies,
That seem her heart's rich thinkings to repeat.
But when the branch is still, her little breast
Swells out in rapture's gushing symphonies ;
And then, against her brown wing softly prest,
The wind comes playing, an enraptured guest ;
This way and that she swings—till gusts arise
More boisterous in their play, then off she flies.

ON THE PICTURE OF A LADY.

SORROW hath made thine eyes more dark and keen,
And set a whiter hue upon thy cheeks,
And round thy pressèd lips drawn anguish-streaks,
And made thy forehead fearfully serene.
Even in thy steady hair her work is seen;
For its still parted darkness—till it breaks
In heavy curls upon thy shoulders—speaks,
Like the stern wave, how hard the storm hath been.
So looked that hapless Lady of the south,
Sweet Isabella, at that dreary part
Of all the passioned hours of her youth
When her green basil pot by brothers' art
Was stolen away: so looked her painèd mouth
In the mute patience of a breaking heart.

NOVEMBER.

YET one smile more, departing, distant Sun!
One mellow smile through the soft vapory air
Ere, o'er the frozen earth, the loud winds run
Or snows are sifted o'er the meadows bare;
One smile on the brown hills and naked trees,
And the dark rocks whose summer wreaths are cast,
And the blue gentian flower, that in the breeze,
Nods lonely, of her beauteous race the last.
Yet a few sunny days in which the bee
Shall murmur by the hedge that skirts the way,
The cricket chirp upon the russet lea,
And man delight to linger in thy ray.
Yet one rich smile, and we will try to bear
The piercing winter frost, and winds, and darkened air.

ON A REMEMBERED PICTURE OF CHRIST.

AN ECCE HOMO BY LEONARDO DA VINCI.

MET that image on a mirthful day
Of youth ; and sinking with a stilled surprise,
The pride of life, before those holy eyes,
In my quick heart died thoughtfully away,
Abashed to mute confession of a sway
Awful though meek ; and now that from the strings
Of my soul's lyre the tempest's mighty wings
Have struck forth tones which then unwakened lay;
Now that around the deep life of my mind
Affections deathless as itself have twined,
Oft does the pale bright vision still float by ;
But more divinely sweet, and speaking now
Of One whose pity, throned on that sad brow,
Sounded all depths of love, grief, death, humanity.

ON FIRST LOOKING INTO CHAPMAN'S 'HOMER.'

MUCH have I travelled in the realms of gold,
And many goodly states and kingdoms seen;
Round many western islands have I been
Which bards in fealty to Apollo hold.
Oft of one wide expanse had I been told
That deep-browed Homer ruled as his demesne:
Yet did I never breathe its pure serene
Till I heard Chapman speak out loud and bold:
Then felt I like some watcher of the skies
When a new planet swims into his ken;
Or like stout Cortez when with eagle eyes
He stared at the Pacific—and all his men
Looked at each other with a wild surmise—
Silent, upon a peak in Darien.

TO HOMER.

STANDING aloof in giant ignorance,
Of thee I hear and of the Cyclades,
As one who sits ashore and longs perchance
To visit dolphin-coral in deep seas.
So thou wast blind !—but then the veil was rent,
For Jove uncurtained Heaven to let thee live,
And Neptune made for thee a spermy tent,
And Pan made sing for thee his forest-hive ;
Aye, on the shores of darkness there is light,
And precipices show untrodden green ;
There is a budding morrow in midnight ;
There is a triple sight in blindness keen ;
Such seeing hadst thou, as it once befel,
To Dian, Queen of Earth, and Heaven, and Hell.

ON THE ELGIN MARBLES.

Y spirit is too weak; mortality
Weighs heavily on me like unwilling sleep,
And each imagined pinnacle and steep
Of godlike hardship tells me I must die
Like a sick eagle looking at the sky.
Yet 'tis a gentle luxury to weep,
That I have not the cloudy winds to keep
Fresh for the opening of the morning's eye.
Such dim-conceived glories of the brain
Bring round the heart an indescribable feud;
So do these wonders a most dizzy pain,
That mingles Grecian grandeur with the rude
Wasting of old Time—with a billowy main
A sun, a shadow of a magnitude.

TO . . .[1]

TIME'S sea hath been five years at its slow ebb,
Long hours have to and fro let creep the sand,
Since I was tangled in thy beauty's web
And snared by the ungloving of thine hand.
And yet I never look on midnight sky
But I behold thine eyes' well memoried light;
I cannot look upon the rose's dye
But to thy cheek my soul doth take its flight;
I cannot look on any budding flower,
But my fond ear, in fancy at thy lips
And hearkening for a love-sound, doth devour
Its sweets in the wrong sense :—Thou dost eclipse
Every delight with sweet remembering,
And grief unto my darling joys dost bring.

[1] A lady whom he saw for some few moments at Vauxhall.

ON A DREAM.

S Hermes once took to his feathers light,
When lulled Argus, baffled, swooned and slept,
So on a Delphic reed, my idle spright,
So played, so charmed, so conquered, so bereft
The dragon-world of all its hundred eyes,
And seeing it asleep, so fled away,
Not to pure Ida with its snow-cold skies,
Nor unto Tempe, where Jove grieved a day,
But to that second circle of sad Hell,
Where in the gust, the whirlwind, and the flaw
Of rain and hail-stones, lovers need not tell
Their sorrows,—pale were the sweet lips I saw,
Pale were the lips I kissed, and fair the form
I floated with, about that melancholy storm.

TO SLEEP.

O SOFT embalmer of the still midnight!
Shutting with careful fingers and benign
Our gloom-pleased eyes, embowered from the light,
Enshaded in forgetfulness divine:
O soothest Sleep! if so it please thee, close,
In midst of this thine hymn, my willing eyes,
Or wait the amen, ere thy poppy throws
Around my bed its lulling charities;
Then save me, or the passèd day will shine
Upon my pillow, breeding many woes;
Save me from curious conscience, that still lords
Its strength, in darkness burrowing like a mole;
Turn the key deftly in the oilèd wards,
And seal the hushèd casket of my soul.

WHY did I laugh to-night? No voice will tell:
  No God, no Demon of severe response,
  Deigns to reply from Heaven or from Hell.
 Then to my human heart I turn at once.
Heart! Thou and I are here sad and alone;
 I say, why did I laugh? O mortal pain!
O Darkness! Darkness! ever must I moan,
 To question Heaven and Hell and Heart in vain.
Why did I laugh? I know this Being's lease,
 My fancy to its utmost blisses spreads;
Yet would I on this very midnight cease
 And the world's gaudy ensigns see in shreds;
Verse, Fame, and Beauty are intense indeed,
But Death intenser—Death is Life's high meed.

BRIGHT star! would I were steadfast as thou
art—
Not in lone splendour hung aloft the night,
And watching, with eternal lids apart,
Like Nature's patient, sleepless Eremite,
The moving waters at their priest-like task
Of pure ablution round earth's human shores,
Or gazing on the new soft fallen mask
Of snow upon the mountains and the moors—

No—yet still steadfast, still unchangeable,
Pillowed upon my fair love's ripening breast
To feel for ever its soft fall and swell,
Awake for ever in a sweet unrest,
Still, still to hear her tender-taken breath,
Half-passionless, and so swoon on to death.

THEY say that thou wert lovely on thy bier,
 More lovely than in life; that when the thrall
 Of earth was loosed, it seemed as though a pall
Of years were lifted, and thou didst appear
Such as of old amidst thy home's calm sphere
 Thou sat'st, a kindly Presence felt by all
 In joy or grief, from morn to evening-fall,
The peaceful Genius of that mansion dear.
Was it the craft of all-persuading Love
 That wrought this marvel? or is Death indeed
A mighty master, gifted from above
  With alchemy benign, to wounded hearts
  Ministering thus, by quaint and subtle arts,
 Strange comfort, whereon after-thought may feed?

ON THE DEATH OF QUEEN CAROLINE.

WHO shall lament to know thy aching head
Hath found its pillow?—that in long repose
Great Death, the noblest of thy kingly foes,
Hath laid thee, and, with sacred veil outspread,
Guards thee from basest insults? Thou hast led
A solitary course,—among the great
A regal hermitess, despoiled of state,
Or mocked and fretted by one tattered shred
Of melancholy grandeur: thou didst wed
Only to be more mournfully alone!
But now, thy sad regalities o'erthrown,
No more an alien from the common fate,
Thou hast one human blessing for thine own—
A place of rest in Nature's kindliest bed.

WHAT was 't awakened first the untried ear
  Of that sole man who was all human kind?—
  Was it the gladsome welcome of the wind,
Stirring the leaves that never yet were sere?
The four mellifluous streams which flowed so near,
  Their lulling murmurs all in one combined?
  The note of bird unnamed? The startled hind
Bursting the brake—in wonder, not in fear,
Of her new lord? Or did the holy ground
  Send forth mysterious melody to greet
  The gracious pressure of immaculate feet?
Did viewless seraphs rustle all around,
  Making sweet music out of air as sweet?
Or his own voice awake him with its sound?

NIGHT.

THE crackling embers on the hearth are dead;
The indoor note of industry is still;
The latch is fast; upon the window-sill
The small birds wait not for their daily bread;
The voiceless flowers—how quietly they shed
Their nightly odours;—and the household rill
Murmurs continuous dulcet sounds that fill
The vacant expectation, and the dread
Of listening night. And haply now she sleeps;
For all the garrulous noises of the air
Are hushed in peace; the soft dew silent weeps,
Like hopeless lovers for a maid so fair:—
Oh! that I were the happy dream that creeps
To her soft heart, to find my image there.

F I have sinned in act, I may repent;
If I have erred in thought, I may disclaim
My silent error, and yet feel no shame;
But if my soul, big with an ill intent,
Guilty in will, by fate be innocent,
Or being bad, yet murmurs at the curse
And incapacity of being worse,
That makes my hungry passion still keep Lent
In keen expectance of a Carnival,—
Where, in all worlds that round the sun revolve
And shed their influence on this passive ball,
Abides a power that can my soul absolve?
Could any sin survive and be forgiven,
One sinful wish would make a hell of heaven.

PRAYER.

THERE is an awful quiet in the air,
  And the sad earth, with moist imploring eye,
  Looks wide and wakeful at the pondering sky,
Like Patience slow subsiding to Despair.
But see, the blue smoke as a voiceless prayer,
  Sole witness of a secret sacrifice,
  Unfolds its tardy wreaths, and multiplies
Its soft chameleon breathings in the rare
Capacious ether,—so it fades away,
  And nought is seen beneath the pendent blue
The undistinguishable waste of day.
  So have I dreamed!—oh may the dream be true!—
  That praying souls are purged from mortal hue,
And grow as pure as He to whom they pray.

LONG time a child, and still a child, when years
Had painted manhood on my cheek, was I;
For yet I lived like one not born to die;
A thriftless prodigal of smiles and tears,
No hope I needed, and I knew no fears.
But sleep, though sweet, is only sleep; and waking,
I waked to sleep no more; at once o'ertaking
The vanguard of my age, with all arrears
Of duty on my back. Nor child, nor man,
Nor youth, nor sage, I find my head is grey,
For I have lost the race I never ran:
A rathe December blights my lagging May;
And still I am a child, though I be old:
Time is my debtor for my years untold.

SILENCE.

THERE is a silence where hath been no sound,
  There is a silence where no sound may be,
  In the cold grave—under the deep deep sea,
Or in wide desert where no life is found,
Which hath been mute, and still must sleep profound;
  No voice is hushed—no life treads silently,
  But clouds and cloudy shadows wander free,
That never spoke, over the idle ground:
But in green ruins, in the desolate walls
  Of antique palaces, where Man hath been,
Though the dun fox, or wild hyæna, calls,
  And owls, that flit continually between,
Shriek to the echo, and the low winds moan,
There the true Silence is, self-conscious and alone.

DEATH.

T is not death, that sometime in a sigh
This eloquent breath shall take its speechless flight;
That sometime these bright stars, that now reply
In sunlight to the sun, shall set in night;
That this warm conscious flesh shall perish quite,
And all life's ruddy springs forget to flow;
That thoughts shall cease, and the immortal sprite
Be lapped in alien clay and laid below;
It is not death to know this,—but to know
That pious thoughts, which visit at new graves
In tender pilgrimage, will cease to go
So duly and so oft,—and when grass waves
Over the past-away, there may be then
No resurrection in the minds of men.

SUBSTANCE AND SHADOW.

THEY do but grope in learning's pedant round
Who on the fantasies of sense bestow
An idol substance, bidding us bow low
Before those shades of being which are found,
Stirring or still, on man's brief trial-ground ;
As if such shapes and modes, which come and go,
Had aught of Truth or Life in their poor show,
To sway or judge, and skill to sain or wound.

Son of immortal seed, high-destined man!
Know thy dread gift,—a creature, yet a cause:
Each mind is its own centre, and it draws
Home to itself, and moulds in its thought's span,
All outward things, the vassals of its will,
Aided by Heaven, by earth unthwarted still.

MELCHIZEDEK.

'Without father, without mother, without descent; having neither beginning of days nor end of life.'

THRICE bless'd are they, who feel their loneliness;
To whom nor voice of friends nor pleasant scene
Brings that on which the saddened heart can lean;
Yea the rich earth, garb'd in her daintiest dress
Of light and joy doth but the more oppress,
Claiming responsive smiles and rapture high;
Till sick at heart, beyond the veil they fly,
Seeking His Presence, who alone can bless.

Such, in strange days, the weapons of Heaven's grace;
When passing o'er the high-born Hebrew line,
He forms the vessel of His vast design;
Fatherless, homeless, reft of age and place,
Severed from earth, and careless of its wreck,
Born through long woe His rare Melchizedek.

ON THE DEATH OF A WORLDLY-MINDED MAN.

HEED not a world that neither thee can keep,
Nor vestige of thee, whatsoe'er thy lot—
Of thee or thine, nor mark when thou art not.
No more!—engulfed within the sounding deep,
Faint and more faint the billowy circles sweep,
And trembling own the shock; then 'tis forgot:
The leaf's still image anchors on the spot,
The wave is in its noonday couch asleep.

We marked the eddying whirlpools close around
Where he had been; but who the path profound—
What thought can follow 'neath the watery floor,
'Mid sights of strangeness and untravelled caves,
Ocean's wild deeps of ever-moving waves,
A boundless, new horizon spreading o'er?

HIDDEN JOYS.

PLEASURES lie thickest where no pleasures seem:
There 's not a leaf that falls upon the ground
But holds some joy, of silence or of sound,
Some sprite begotten of a summer dream.
The very meanest things are made supreme
With innate ecstasy. No grain of sand
But moves a bright and million-peopled land,
And hath its Edens and its Eves, I deem.
For Love, though blind himself, a curious eye
Hath lent me, to behold the hearts of things,
And touched mine ear with power. Thus, far or nigh,
Minute or mighty, fixed or free with wings,
Delight from many a nameless covert sly
Peeps sparkling, and in tones familiar sings.

TO ROBERT SOUTHEY.

THIS Book, though it should travel far and wide
As ever unripe Author's quick conceit
Could feign his page dispersed, should nowhere meet
A friendlier censor than by Greta's side,
A warmer welcome than at Skiddaw's feet.
Unhappily infrequent in the land
Is now the sage seclusion, the retreat
Sacred to letters: but let this command
Fitting acknowledgment,—that time and tide
Saw never yet embellished with more grace
Outward and inward, with more charms allied,
With honours more attended, man or place,
Than where by Greta's silver current sweet
Learning still keeps one calm sequestered seat.

WELLINGTON.

NOT only that thy puissant arm could bind
The tyrant of a world, and, conquering Fate,
Enfranchise Europe, do I deem thee great;
But that in all thy actions I do find
Exact propriety: no gusts of mind
Fitful and wild, but that continuous state
Of ordered impulse mariners await
In some benignant and enriching wind,—
The breath ordained of Nature. Thy calm mien
Recalls old Rome, as much as thy high deed;
Duty thine only idol, and serene
When all are troubled; in the utmost need
Prescient; thy country's servant ever seen,
Yet sovereign of thyself, whate'er may speed.

THE OLD BRIDGE AT FLORENCE.

TADDEO Gaddi built me. I am old,
Five centuries old. I plant my foot of stone
Upon the Arno, as St. Michael's own
Was planted on the dragon. Fold by fold
Beneath me as it struggles, I behold
Its glistening scales. Twice hath it overthrown
My kindred and companions. Me alone
It moveth not, but is by me controlled.
I can remember when the Medici
Were driven from Florence; longer still ago
The final wars of Ghibelline and Guelf.
Florence adorns me with her jewelry;
And when I think that Michael Angelo
Hath leaned on me, I glory in myself.

THE BURIAL OF THE POET.

RICHARD HENRY DANA.

IN the old churchyard of his native town,
And in the ancestral tomb beside the wall,
We laid him in the sleep that comes to all,
And left him to his rest and his renown.
The snow was falling as if Heaven dropped down
White flowers of Paradise to strew his pall :—
The dead around him seemed to wake, and call
His name, as worthy of so white a crown.
And now the moon is shining on the scene,
And the broad sheet of snow is written o'er
With shadows cruciform of leafless trees,
As once the winding-sheet of Saladin
With chapters of the Koran ; but, ah ! more
Mysterious and triumphant signs are these.

NATURE.

AS a fond mother, when the day is o'er,
Leads by the hand her little child to bed,
Half willing, half reluctant to be led,
And leave his broken playthings on the floor,
Still gazing at them through the open door,
Nor wholly reassured and comforted
By promises of others in their stead,
Which, though more splendid, may not please him more:

So Nature deals with us, and takes away
Our playthings one by one, and by the hand
Leads us to rest so gently, that we go
Scarce knowing if we wished to go or stay,
Being too full of sleep to understand
How far the unknown transcends the what we know.

VESUVIUS.

AS when unto a mother, having chid
    Her child in anger, there have straight ensued
    Repentings for her quick and angry mood,
That she would fain see all its traces hid
Quite out of sight,—even so has Nature bid
  Fair flowers, that on the scarred earth she has strewed,
  To blossom; and called up the taller wood
To cover what she ruined and undid.
Oh! and her mood of anger did not last
  More than an instant; but her work of peace,
    Restoring and repairing, comforting
  The earth her stricken child, will never cease:
For that was her strange work, and quickly past;
    To this, her genial toil, no end the years shall bring.

A WRETCHED thing it were to have our heart
  Like a broad highway or a populous street,
  Where every idle thought has leave to meet,
Pause or pass on as in an open mart;
Or like some road-side pool, which no nice art
  Has guarded that the cattle may not beat
  And foul it with a multitude of feet,
Till of the heavens it can give back no part.
But keep thou thine a holy solitude,
  For He who would walk there would walk alone;
He who would drink there must be first endued
  With single right to call that stream his own;
Keep thou thine heart close fastened, unrevealed,
A fencèd garden and a fountain sealed.

THE OCEAN.

THE Ocean at the bidding of the Moon,
For ever changes with his restless tide;
Hung shoreward now, to be regathered soon
With kingly pauses of reluctant pride,
And semblance of return. Anon from home
He issues forth again, high-ridged and free,
The seething hiss of his tumultuous foam
Like armies whispering where great echoes be!
Oh, leave me here upon this beach to rove,
Mute listener to that sound so grand and lone—
A glorious sound, deep-drawn and strongly thrown,
And reaching those on mountain heights above;
To British ears, as who shall scorn to own,
A tutelar fond voice, a saviour-tone of love.

THE BUOY-BELL.

HOW like the leper, with his own sad cry
Enforcing his own solitude, it tolls!
That lonely bell set in the rushing shoals,
To warn us from the place of jeopardy!
O friend of man! sore-vexed by Ocean's power,
The changing tides wash o'er thee day by day;
Thy trembling mouth is filled with bitter spray,
Yet still thou ringest on from hour to hour;
High is thy mission, though thy lot is wild—
To be in danger's realm a guardian sound;
In seamen's dreams a pleasant part to bear,
And earn their blessing as the year goes round;
And strike the key-note of each grateful prayer,
Breathed in their distant homes by wife or child.

THE PRISONER.

HIS was a chamber in the topmost tower—
A small unsightly cell with grated bars;
And wearily went on each irksome hour
Of dim captivity and moody cares;
Against such visitants he was not strong,
But sat with laden heart and brow of woe;
And every morn he heard the stir and song
Of birds in royal gardens far below,
Telling of bowers and dewy lawns unseen,
Drenched with the silver stream that night had shed,
Part blossom-white, part exquisitely green,
By little warblers roamed and tenanted,
Blending their glad wild notes to greet the sheen
Of the May Dawn, that gleamed upon his bed.

THE TRAVELLER AND HIS WIFE'S RINGLET.

I HAVE a circlet of thy sunny hair,
A light from home, a blessing to mine eyes;
Though grave and mournful thoughts will often rise,
As I behold it mutely glistening there,
So still, so passive! like a treasure's key,
Unconscious of the dreams it doth compel,
Of gems and gold, high-piled in secret cell,
Too royal for a vulgar gaze to see!
If they were stolen, the key could never tell;
If thou wert dead, what should thy ringlet say?
It shows the same, betide thee ill or well,
Smiling in love, or shrouded in decay;
It cannot darken for dead Isabel,
Nor blanch if thy young head grew white to-day.

THE LATTICE AT SUNRISE.

AS on my bed at dawn I mused and prayed,
I saw my lattice prankt upon the wall,
The flaunting leaves and flitting birds withal—
A sunny phantom interlaced with shade;
'Thanks be to heaven!' in happy mood I said,
'What sweeter aid my matins could befall
Than this fair glory from the East hath made?
What holy sleights hath God, the Lord of all,
To bid us feel and see! we are not free
To say we see not, for the glory comes
Nightly and daily, like the flowing sea;
His lustre pierceth through the midnight glooms;
And, at prime hour, behold! He follows me
With golden shadows to my secret rooms!'

SILENCE.

THERE are some qualities—some incorporate things,
That have a double life, which thus is made
A type of that twin entity which springs
From matter and light, evinced in solid and shade.
There is a two-fold Silence—sea and shore—
Body and soul. One dwells in lonely places,
Newly with grass o'ergrown; some solemn graces,
Some human memories and tearful lore,
Render him terrorless; his name's 'No More.'
He is the corporate Silence: dread him not!
No power hath he of evil in himself;
But should some urgent fate (untimely lot!)
Bring thee to meet his shadow (nameless elf,
That haunteth the lone regions where hath trod
No foot of man), commend thyself to God!

PREFATORY SONNET TO THE 'NINETEENTH CENTURY.'

THOSE that of late had flitted far and fast
To touch all shores, now leaving to the skill
Of others their old craft seaworthy still,
Have chartered this; where, mindful of the past,
Our true co-mates regather round the mast;
Of diverse tongue, but with a common will
Here in this roaring moon of daffodil
And crocus, to put forth and brave the blast;
For some, descending from the sacred peak
Of hoar high-templed Faith, have leagued again
Their lot with ours to rove the world about;
And some are wilder comrades, sworn to seek
If any golden harbour be for men
In seas of Death and sunless gulfs of Doubt.

MONTENEGRO.

THEY rose to where their sovran eagle sails,
They kept their faith, their freedom, on the height,
Chaste, frugal, savage, armed by day and night
Against the Turk; whose inroad nowhere scales
Their headlong passes, but his footstep fails,
And red with blood the Crescent reels from fight
Before their dauntless hundreds, in prone flight
By thousands down the crags and through the vales.

O smallest among peoples! rough rock-throne
Of Freedom! warriors beating back the swarm
Of Turkish Islam for five hundred years,
Great Tsernagora! never since thine own
Black ridges drew the cloud and brake the storm
Has breathed a race of mightier mountaineers.

THE SOUL'S EXPRESSION.

WITH stammering lips and insufficient sound,
I strive and struggle to deliver right
The music of my nature, day and night
With dream and thought and feeling interwound,
And inly answering all the senses round
With octaves of a mystic depth and height
Which step out grandly to the infinite
From the dark edges of the sensual ground.
This song of soul I struggle to outbear
Through portals of the sense, sublime and whole,
And utter all myself into the air;
But if I did it,—as the thunder-roll
Breaks its own cloud, my flesh would perish there,
Before that dread apocalypse of soul.

PERPLEXED MUSIC.

EXPERIENCE, like a pale musician, holds
A dulcimer of patience in his hand,
Whence harmonies we cannot understand,
Of God's will in His worlds, the strain unfolds
In sad, perplexèd minors: deathly colds
Fall on us while we hear, and countermand
Our sanguine heart back from the fancy-land
With nightingales in visionary wolds.
We murmur, 'Where is any certain tune
Or measured music in such notes as these?'
But angels, leaning from the golden seat,
Are not so minded; their fine ear hath won
The issue of completed cadences,
And, smiling down the stars, they whisper—SWEET.

TEARS.

THANK God, bless God, all ye who suffer not
More grief than ye can weep for. That is well—
That is light grieving! lighter none befell
Since Adam forfeited the primal lot.
Tears! what are tears? The babe weeps in its cot,
The mother singing; at her marriage-bell
The bride weeps, and before the oracle
Of high-faned hills the poet has forgot
Such moisture on his cheeks. Thank God for grace,
Ye who weep only! If, as some have done,
Ye grope tear-blinded in a desert place
And touch but tombs,—look up! those tears will run
Soon in long rivers down the lifted face,
And leave the vision clear for stars and sun.

WORK.

WHAT are we set on earth for? Say, to toil;
Nor seek to leave the tending of the vines
For all the heat o' the day, till it declines,
And Death's mild curfew shall from work assoil.
God did anoint thee with His odorous oil
To wrestle, not to reign; and He assigns
All thy tears over, like pure crystallines,
For younger fellow-workers of the soil
To wear for amulets. So others shall
Take patience, labour, to their heart and hand,
From thy hand and thy heart and thy brave cheer,
And God's grace fructify through thee to all.
The least flower with a brimming cup may stand,
And share its dew-drop with another near.

SONNETS FROM THE PORTUGUESE.

(XIV)

F thou must love me, let it be for nought
Except for love's sake only. Do not say
'I love her for her smile...her look...her way
Of speaking gently, . . . for a trick of thought
That falls in well with mine, and certes brought
A sense of pleasant ease on such a day ;'—
For these things in themselves, Beloved, may
Be changed, or change for thee,—and love so wrought,
May be unwrought so. Neither love me for
Thine own dear pity's wiping my cheeks dry,—
A creature might forget to weep who bore
Thy comfort long, and lose thy love thereby !
But love me for love's sake, that evermore
Thou mayest love on, through love's eternity.

(XVIII)

I NEVER gave a lock of hair away
To a man, Dearest, except this to thee,
Which now upon my fingers thoughtfully
I ring out to the full brown length and say
'Take it.' My day of youth went yesterday;
My hair no longer bounds to my foot's glee,
Nor plant I it from rose or myrtle tree,
As girls do, any more: it only may
Now shade on two pale cheeks the mark of tears,
Taught drooping from the head that hangs aside
Through sorrow's trick. I thought the funeral shears
Would take this first, but Love is justified,—
Take it thou,—finding pure, from all those years,
The kiss my mother left here when she died.

(xx)

BELOVED, my Beloved, when I think
That thou wast in the world a year ago,
What time I sat alone here in the snow
And saw no footprint, heard the silence sink
No moment at thy voice, . . . but, link by link,
Went counting all my chains, as if that so
They never could fall off at any blow
Struck by thy possible hand . . . why, thus I drink
Of life's great cup of wonder! Wonderful,
Never to feel thee thrill the day or night
With personal act or speech,—nor ever cull
Some prescience of thee with the blossoms white
Thou sawest growing! Atheists are as dull,
Who cannot guess God's presence out of sight.

(xxxv)

IF I leave all for thee, wilt thou exchange
And be all to me? Shall I never miss
Home-talk and blessing and the common kiss
That comes to each in turn, nor count it strange,
When I look up, to drop on a new range
Of walls and floors . . . another home than this?
Nay, wilt thou fill that place by me which is
Filled by dead eyes too tender to know change?
That 's hardest. If to conquer love has tried,
To conquer grief, tries more . . . as all things prove;
For grief indeed is love and grief beside.
Alas, I have grieved so I am hard to love.
Yet love me—wilt thou? Open thine heart wide
And fold within the wet wings of thy dove.

HAPPINESS.

I.

BECAUSE the Few with signal virtue crowned,
The heights and pinnacles of human mind,
Sadder and wearier than the rest are found,
Wish not thy Soul less wise or less refined.
True that the small delights which every day
Cheer and distract the pilgrim are not theirs;
True that, though free from Passion's lawless sway,
A loftier being brings severer cares.
Yet they have special pleasures, even Mirth,
By those undreamt-of who have only trod
Life's valley smooth; and if the rolling earth
To their nice ear have many a painful tone,
They know, Man does not live by Joy alone,
But by the presence of the power of God.

II.

SPLENDOUR amid glooms,—a sunny thread
Woven into a tapestry of cloud,—
A merry child a-playing with the shroud
That lies upon a breathless mother's bed,—
A garland on the front of one new-wed,
Trembling and weeping while her troth is vowed,—
A schoolboy's laugh that rises light and loud
In licensed freedom from ungentle dread;
These are ensamples of the Happiness
For which our nature fits us; More and Less
Are parts of all things to the mortal given,
Of Love, Joy, Truth, and Beauty. Perfect Light
Would dazzle, not illuminate our sight,—
From Earth it is enough to glimpse at Heaven.

JUMNOTREE.

SHARP, clear, and crystalline, cleaving the sky
In twain, it towers for ever and alone,
Save that about its feet the tall hills lie,
Like slaves around some mighty despot's throne;
While evermore, beneath its cold stern eye,
The short-lived centuries have come and flown,
And stars that round its head untiring fly,
Confess its ancient glories as their own.
The eagles shun it in their highest flight,
The clouds lie basking 'neath its eminence;
Naught nears it but thin air and heaven's sweet light,
Nor not a sound for ever cometh thence,
Save of some avalanche from its summit riven,
Or thunder-tempest on its breakers driven.

THE ORIGIN OF EVIL.

I.

THE origin of evil?—good my friend,
  Ask him who helps my vegetable needs,
  The gardener there, the origin of weeds;
He'll turn about and stare to comprehend
What thing you mean. 'The weeds,' he says, 'are there
  No doubt with very proper right to grow,
And I with them have equal right to care
  For flowery fragrance and for blooming show.'
This man is wise; and you, what thing are you?
  A thing of idle dreams and fancies crude;
  Evil exists, that you may make it good,
Else had the Saints on Earth scant work to do.
  What would you have?—in Paradise no doubt
  Weeds grandly grew, and Adam plucked them out.

II.

THE origin of Evil? good my friend,
  To ask such questions proves thee far from wise;
  No mightiest man that walks beneath the skies
Hath plumb to measure, or device to mend,
The vasty Universe. If thou wouldst know
  Whence Evil comes, first say what evil means,
  And if this pictured pomp of shifting scenes
Which men call life, a many-mingling show,
Was made for your mere pleasure or for mine.
  Cease foolish questions; here for me and you
  Close by the door is fruitful work to do;
Accept the task, and own the work divine;
  Sow, plant, or build, drain fields, or cleave the clod,
  But spend no breath in arguing with God.

HIGHLAND SOLITUDE.

IN the lone glen the silver lake doth sleep;
Sleeps the white cloud upon the sheer black hill;
All moorland sounds a solemn silence keep;
I only hear the tiny trickling rill
'Neath the red moss. Athwart the dim grey pall
That veils the day a dusky fowl may fly;
But on this bleak brown moor, if thou shalt call
For men, a spirit will sooner make reply.
Come hither thou whose agile talk doth flit
From theme to theme, and tempt the pensive mood;
Converse with men makes sharp the glittering wit,
But God to man doth speak in solitude.
Come, sit thee down upon this old grey stone;
Men learn to think, and feel, and pray, alone.

RISE, said the Master, come unto the feast;—
  She heard the call and rose with willing feet;
  But thinking it not otherwise than meet
For such a bidding to put on her best,
She is gone from us for a few short hours
  Into her bridal closet, there to wait
  For the unfolding of the palace gate,
That gives her entrance to the blissful bowers.
We have not seen her yet, though we have been
  Full often to her chamber door, and oft
Have listened underneath the postern green,
  And laid fresh flowers, and whispered short and soft;
But she hath made no answer; and the day
From the clear west is fading far away.

MELANCHOLY.

THERE sat a maiden 'neath a regal tower
Girt with a forest of great oaks and pines;
It seemed a lodge of some high conqueror
In the old days; and round it creeping vines
Grew wildly, that no more men drank of now;
And in the topmost arch there was a bell
That with the wind did vibrate;—vague and low
Sped o'er the hills its modulated swell.
Palely she sat, and at her side were things
Of strange device to measure earth and stars,
And a small, quiet genius, with his wings
Unfolded, and his eyes still fixed on hers—
Men uttered not her queenly name; but she
Had graved it in the dust, 'Melancholie.'

THE PINE WOODS.

WE stand upon the moorish mountain side,
From age to age, a solemn company;
There are no voices in our paths, but we
Hear the great whirlwinds roaring loud and wide;
And like the sea-waves have our boughs replied
From the beginning, to their stormy glee:
The thunder rolls above us, and some tree
Smites with his bolt, yet doth the race abide
Answering all times; but joyous, when the sun
Glints on the peaks that clouds no longer bear;
And the young shoots to flourish have begun;
And the quick seeds through the blue odorous air
From the expanding cones fall one by one;
And silence as in temples dwelleth there.

HE garden trees are busy with the shower
That fell ere sunset: now methinks they talk,
Lowly and sweetly as befits the hour,
One to another down the grassy walk.
Hark the laburnum from his opening flower
This cherry-creeper greets in whisper light,
While the grim fir, rejoicing in the night,
Hoarse murmurs to the murmuring sycamore.
What shall I deem their converse? Would they hail
The wild grey light that fronts yon massive cloud,
Or the half-bow, rising like pillared fire?
Or are they sighing faintly for desire
That with May dawn their leaves may be o'erflowed,
And dews about their feet may never fail?

EVEN as yon lamp within my vacant room
  With arduous flame disputes the doubtful night,
  And can with its involuntary light
But lifeless things that near it stand illume ;
Yet all the while it doth itself consume,
  And ere the sun hath reached his morning height
  With courier beams that greet the shepherd's sight,
There where its life arose must be its tomb :—

So wastes my life away. Perforce confined
  To common things, a limit to its sphere,
It gleams on worthless trifles undesigned
  With fainter ray each hour imprisoned here.
Alas to know that the consuming mind
  Must leave its lamp cold ere the sun appear !

ON THE BIRTH OF THOMAS CARLYLE'S GREAT-NEPHEW,
2D JUNE 1880.

COMING and going: still one Norn descends
To Urda's fount with empty urn, while one
Rises again life-laden to the sun,
And the great Tree still nigher heaven tends
Fresher and lovelier, as the new time lends
New energies. O welcome, latest come!
Inheritor and priest when we 've gone home,
Welcome thou dreadest gift the good God sends.

Dreadest and dearest, lo, the innocent hand
Lying within its mother's, what command
May it yet hold! Hear the tongue's speechless cry,
May it not utter yet the inspirèd word
Nations have waited for, the which when heard,
Shall clear, like lightning, the world's future sky!

THE ROBIN'S OCTOBER SONG.

THAT carol to the cold and misty morn,
  That ending autumn-song, that short-lived song,
  O robin! I know well, so sharp and strong,
As do those trembling groves already shorn
And yellowing. O brief sweet song! so lorn
  Of gladness; all these leaves, from twig to stem,
  Tremble as if dead fingers counted them:—
To sing such song men too were surely born.

And this it is: the most desired of Gods
  Is waxen weak, and all his children too,
  Even the sun; that wide-winged spectre flew
    Faster, and now hath caught him by the hair.
Let us contend no more against the rods,
    But sing our last song, and descend the stair.

THE UNIVERSE VOID.

EVOLVING worlds, revolving systems, yea,
  Revolving firmaments, nor there we end:
  Systems of firmaments revolving, send
Our thought across the Infinite astray,
Gasping and lost and terrified, the day
  Of life, the goodly interests of home,
  Shrivelled to nothing; that unbounded dome
Pealing still on, in blind fatality.

No rest is there for our soul's wingèd feet,
  She must return for shelter to her ark—
The body, fair, frail, death-born, incomplete;
  And let her bring this truth back from the dark,
Life is self-centred, man is nature's god,
Space, time, are but the walls of his abode.

RT thou already weary of the way,
Thou who hast yet but half the way gone o'er?
Get up, and lift thy burthen; lo, before
Thy feet the road goes stretching far away.
If thou already faint, who hast but come
Through half thy pilgrimage, with fellows gay,
Love, youth, and hope, under the rosy bloom
And temperate airs of early breaking day—
Look yonder, how the heavens stoop and gloom;
There cease the trees to shade, the flowers to spring,
And the angels leave thee. What wilt thou become
Through yon drear stretch of dismal wandering,
Lonely and dark? I shall take courage, friend,
For comes not every step more near the end.

COUNT each affliction, whether light or grave,
God's messenger sent down to thee; do thou
With courtesy receive him; rise and bow
And, ere his shadow pass thy threshold, crave
Permission first his heavenly feet to lave;
Then lay before him all thou hast; allow
No cloud of passion to usurp thy brow,
Or mar thy hospitality; no wave
Of mortal tumult to obliterate
The soul's marmoreal calmness: Grief should be
Like joy, majestic, equable, sedate;
Confirming, cleansing, raising, making free;
Strong to consume small troubles; to commend
Great thoughts, grave thoughts, thoughts lasting to the end.

FOR we the mighty mountain plains have trod
Both in the glow of sunset and sunrise;
And lighted by the moon of southern skies!
The snow-white torrent of the thundering flood
We two have watched together. In the wood
We two have felt the warm tears dim our eyes
While zephyrs softer than an infant's sighs
Ruffled the light air of our solitude!

O Earth, maternal Earth, and thou, O Heaven,
And Night first-born, who now, e'en now, dost waken
The host of stars, thy constellated train!
Tell me if those can ever be forgiven,
Those abject, who together have partaken
These Sacraments of Nature—and in vain?

IN MEMORY OF SIR WILLIAM ROWAN HAMILTON.

FRIEND of past years, the holy and the blest,
When all my day shone out, a long sunrise;
When aspirations seemed but sympathies,
In such familiar nearness were they dressed;
When Song, with swan-like plumes and starry crest,
O'er-circled earth, and beat against the skies,
And fearless Science raised her reverent eyes
From heaven to heaven, that each its God confessed
With homage ever widening! Friend beloved!
From me those days are passed; yet still, oh, still,
This night my heart with influx strange they fill
Of beaming memories from my vanished youth:
On thee—the temporal veil by Death removed—
Rests the great Vision of Eternal Truth!

January 10, 1881.

DEDICATION TO *FESTUS.*

MY Father! unto thee to whom I owe
All that I am, all that I have and can;
Who madest me in thyself the sum of man
In all its generous aims and powers to know,
These first-fruits bring I; nor do thou forego
Marking when I the boyish feat began,
Which numbers now near three years from its plan,
Not twenty summers had imbrowned my brow.
Life is at blood-heat every page doth prove.
Bear with it. Nature means Necessity.
If here be aught which thou canst love, it springs
Out of the hope that I may earn that love
More unto me than immortality;
Or to have strung my harp with golden strings.

THE STREET.

THEY pass me by like shadows, crowds on crowds,
  Dim ghosts of men, that hover to and fro,
Hugging their bodies round them like thin shrouds,
  Wherein their souls were buried long ago:
They trampled on their youth, and faith, and love,
  They cast their hope of human-kind away,
With Heaven's clear messages they madly strove,
  And conquered,—and their spirits turned to clay:
Lo! how they wander round the world, their grave,
  Whose ever-gaping maw by such is fed,
Gibbering at living men, and idly rave,
  'We only truly live, but ye are dead.'
Alas! poor fools, the anointed eye may trace
A dead soul's epitaph in every face!

HIGH SUMMER.

NEVER wholly feel that summer is high,
However green the trees or loud the birds,
However movelessly eye-winking herds
Stand in field ponds, or under large trees lie,
Till I do climb all cultured pastures by,
That, hedged by hedgerows studiously trim,
Smile like a lady's face with lace laced prim,
And on some moor or hill that seeks the sky
Lonely and nakedly,—utterly lie down,
And feel the sunshine throbbing on body and limb,
My drowsy brain in pleasant drunkenness swim,
Each rising thought sink back and dreamily drown,
Smiles creep o'er my face, and smother my lips, and cloy,
Each muscle sink to itself, and separately enjoy.

BROTHER AND SISTER.

(1)

CANNOT choose but think upon the time
  When our two lives grew like two buds that kiss
At lightest thrill from the bee's swinging chime,
  Because the one so near the other is.
He was the elder, and a little man
  Of forty inches, bound to show no dread,
And I the girl that puppy-like now ran,
  Now lagged behind my brother's larger tread.
I held him wise, and when he talked to me
  Of snakes and birds, and which God loved the best,
I thought his knowledge marked the boundary
  Where men grew blind, though angels knew the rest.
If he said 'Hush!' I tried to hold my breath;
Wherever he said 'Come!' I stepped in faith.

WORLDLY PLACE.

*VEN in a palace, life may be led well!*
So spake the imperial sage, purest of men,
Marcus Aurelius.—But the stifling den
Of common life, where, crowded up pell-mell,
Our freedom for a little bread we sell,
And drudge under some foolish master's ken,
Who rates us, if we peer outside our pen—
Matched with a palace, is not this a hell?—
Even in a palace! On his truth sincere,
Who spoke those words, no shadow ever came;
And when my ill-schooled spirit is aflame
Some nobler, ampler stage of life to win,
I'll stop and say: 'There were no succour here!
The aids to noble life are all within.'

EAST AND WEST.

IN the bare midst of Anglesey they show
Two springs which close by one another play,
And, 'Thirteen hundred years agone,' they say,
'Two saints met often where those waters flow.
One came from Penmon westward, and a glow
Whitened his face from the sun's fronting ray;
Eastward the other, from the dying day—
And he with unsunned face did always go.'
Seiriol the Bright, *Kybi the Dark!* men said.
The seër from the East was then in light;
The seër from the West was then in shade.
Ah! now 'tis changed. In conquering sunshine bright
The man of the bold West now comes arrayed;
He of the mystic East is touched with night.

EAST LONDON.

'TWAS August, and the fierce sun overhead
Smote on the squalid streets of Bethnal Green,
And the pale weaver, through his windows seen
In Spitalfields, looked thrice dispirited ;
I met a preacher there I knew, and said :
'Ill and o'erworked, how fare you in this scene?'
'Bravely!' said he ; 'for I of late have been
Much cheered with thoughts of Christ, *the living bread.*'
O human soul! as long as thou canst so
Set up a mark of everlasting light,
Above the howling senses' ebb and flow,
To cheer thee, and to right thee if thou roam,
Not with lost toil thou labourest through the night!
Thou mak'st the heaven thou hop'st indeed thy home.

'TIMOR MORTIS CONTURBAT ME.'

COULD I have sung one Song that should survive
The singer's voice, and in my country's heart
Find loving echo—evermore a part
Of all her sweetest memories; could I give
One great Thought to the People, that should prove
The spring of noble action in their hour
Of darkness, or control their headlong power
With the firm reins of Justice and of Love;
Could I have traced one Form that should express
The sacred mystery that underlies
All Beauty, and through man's enraptured eyes
Teach him how beautiful is Holiness,—
I had not feared thee. But to yield my breath,
Life's Purpose unfulfilled!—This is thy sting, O Death!

TO THE MIDNIGHT WIND.

FROM what bleak wastes of utmost loneliness,—
What desolate steeps of misery,—what drear
Caverns of black bewilderment and fear,
Bring'st thou those tones of measureless distress,
Weird wind that shriekest in the midnight gloom
Thine anguished litany ;—as 't were the prayer
Of the World's angel in his strong despair
O'er her mad millions rushing on their doom ;—
As 't were the moan of Time's woe-weary waves
That o'er Eternity's untroubled deep,
Freighted with drowning souls, for ever sweep ;—
As 't were the cry from unremembered graves
Of hopes long dead ?—Ah ! prayer, and moan, and cry,
They are but echoes, heart, of thine own agony.

Y childhood was a vision heavenly wrought;
High joys of which I sometimes dream, yet fail
To recollect sufficient to bewail,
And now for ever seek, came then unsought:
But thoughts denying feeling, every thought
Some buried feeling's ghost, a spirit pale,
Sprang up, and wordy nothings could prevail
And juggle with my soul; since, better taught,
The Christian's apprehension, light that solves
Doubt without logic, rose in logic's room;
Sweet faith came back, sweet faith that hope involves,
And joys, like stars, which, though they not illume
This mortal night, have glory that dissolves
And strikes to quick transparence all its gloom.

AH, God! the world needs many hours to make;
  Nor hast thou ceased the making of it yet,
  But wilt be working on when Death hath set
A new mound in some churchyard for my sake.
On flow the centuries without a break.
  Uprise the mountains, ages without let.
  The mosses suck the rock's breast, rarely wet.
Years more than past the young earth yet will take.
But in the dumbness of the rolling time,
  No veil of silence will encompass me—
  Thou wilt not once forget, and let me be:
I easier think that Thou, as I my rhyme,
Wouldst rise, and with a tenderness sublime
  Unfold a world, that I, Thy child, might see.

TO A FRIEND RECENTLY LOST.

T. T.

WHEN I remember, Friend, whom lost I call
Because a man beloved is taken hence,
The tender humour and the fire of sense
In your good eyes: how full of heart for all,
And chiefly for the weaker by the wall,
You bore that light of sane benevolence:
Then see I round you Death his shadows dense
Divide, and at your feet his emblems fall.
For surely are you one with the white host,
Spirits, whose memory is our vital air,
Through the great love of earth they had: lo, these,
Like beams that throw the path on tossing seas,
Can bid us feel we keep them in the ghost,
Partakers of a strife they joyed to share.

STILL-BORN LOVE.

THE hour which might have been yet might not be,
Which man's and woman's heart conceived and bore
Yet whereof life was barren,—on what shore
Bides it the breaking of Time's weary sea?
Bondchild of all consummate joys set free,
It somewhere sighs and serves, and mute before
The house of Love, hears through the echoing door
His hours elect in choral consonancy.

But lo! what wedded souls now hand in hand
Together tread at last the immortal strand
With eyes where burning memory lights love home?
Lo! how the little outcast hour has turned
And leaped to them and in their faces yearned:
'I am your child! O parents, ye have come!'

KNOWN IN VAIN.

AS two whose love, first foolish, widening scope,
Knows suddenly, to music high and soft,
The Holy of holies; who because they scoffed
Are now amazed with shame, nor dare to cope
With the whole truth aloud, lest heaven should ope;
Yet, at their meetings, laugh not as they laughed
In speech; nor speak at length; but sitting oft
Together, within hopeless sight of hope
For hours are silent:—So it happeneth
Where Work and Will awake too late, to gaze
After their life sailed by, and hold their breath.
Ah! who shall dare to search through what sad maze
Thenceforth their incommunicable ways
Follow the desultory feet of Death.

LOST DAYS.

THE lost days of my life until to-day,
  What were they, could I see them on the street
  Lie as they fell? Would they be ears of wheat
Sown once for food, but trodden into clay?
Or golden coins squandered and still to pay?
  Or drops of blood dabbling the guilty feet?
  Or such spilt water as in dreams must cheat
The undying throats of Hell, athirst alway?

I do not see them here; but after death
  God knows I know the faces I shall see,
Each one a murdered self, with low last breath.
  'I am thyself,—what hast thou done to me?'
'And I—and I—thyself' (lo! each one saith),
  'And thou thyself to all eternity!'

RALEIGH'S CELL IN THE TOWER.

HERE writ was the World's History by his hand
Whose steps knew all the earth; albeit his world
In these few piteous paces then was furled.
Here daily, hourly, have his proud feet spanned
This smaller speck than the receding land
Had ever shown his ships; what time he hurled
Abroad o'er new-found regions spiced and pearled
His country's high dominion and command.

Here dwelt two spheres. The vast terrestrial zone
His spirit traversed; and that spirit was
Itself the zone celestial, round whose birth
The planets played within the zodiac's girth;
Till hence, through unjust death unfeared, did pass
His spirit to the only land unknown.

MARY MAGDALENE AT THE DOOR OF SIMON THE PHARISEE.

(FOR A DRAWING.)[1]

'WHY wilt thou cast the roses from thy hair?
Nay, be thou all a rose,—wreath, lips, and cheek.
Nay, not this house,—that banquet-house we seek;
See how they kiss and enter; come thou there.
This delicate day of love we two will share
Till at our ear love's whispering night shall speak.
What, sweet one, hold'st thou still the foolish freak?
Nay, when I kiss thy feet they'll leave the stair.'

'Oh loose me! See'st thou not my Bridegroom's face
That draws me to Him? For His feet my kiss,
My hair, my tears He craves to-day:—and oh!
What words can tell what other day and place
Shall see me clasp those blood-stained feet of His?
He needs me, calls me, loves me: let me go!'

[1] In the drawing Mary has left a procession of revellers, and is ascending by a sudden impulse the steps of the house where she sees Christ. Her lover has followed her and is trying to turn her back.

TRUE WOMAN.

I.—HERSELF.

TO be a sweetness more desired than Spring;
A bodily beauty more acceptable
Than the wild rose-tree's arch that crowns the fell;
To be an essence more environing
Than wine's drained juice; a music ravishing
More than the passionate pulse of Philomel;—
To be all this 'neath one soft bosom's swell
That is the flower of life:—how strange a thing!

How strange a thing to be what Man can know
But as a sacred secret! Heaven's own screen
Hides her soul's purest depth and loveliest glow;
Closely withheld, as all things most unseen,—
The wave-bowered pearl,—the heart-shaped seal of green
That flecks the snowdrop underneath the snow.

II.—HER LOVE.

SHE loves him; for her infinite soul is Love,
And he her lodestar. Passion in her is
A glass facing his fire, where the bright bliss
Is mirrored, and the heat returned. Yet move
That glass, a stranger's amorous flame to prove,
And it shall turn, by instant contraries,
Ice to the moon; while her pure fire to his
For whom it burns, clings close i' the heart's alcove.

Lo! they are one. With wifely breast to breast
And circling arms, she welcomes all command
Of love,—her soul to answering ardours fann'd:
Yet as morn springs or twilight sinks to rest,
Ah! who shall say she deems not loveliest
The hour of sisterly sweet hand-in-hand?

III.—HER HEAVEN.

F to grow old in Heaven is to grow young,
(As the Seer saw and said,) then blest were he
With youth for evermore, whose heaven should be
True Woman, she whom these weak notes have sung.
Here and hereafter,—choir-strains of her tongue,—
Sky-spaces of her eyes,—sweet signs that flee
About her soul's immediate sanctuary,—
Were Paradise all uttermost worlds among.

The sunrise blooms and withers on the hill
Like any hill-flower; and the noblest troth
Dies here to dust. Yet shall Heaven's promise clothe
Even yet those lovers who have cherished still
This test for love:—in every kiss sealed fast
To feel the first kiss and forebode the last.

DEMOCRACY DOWNTRODDEN.

HOW long, O Lord?—The voice is sounding still:
Not only heard beneath the altar-stone,
Not heard of John Evangelist alone
In Patmos. It doth cry aloud and will
Between the earth's end and earth's end, until
The day of the great reckoning—bone for bone,
And blood for righteous blood, and groan for groan:
Then shall it cease on the air with a sudden thrill;
Not slowly growing fainter if the rod
Strikes here or there amid the evil throng,
Or one oppressor's hand is stayed and numbs;
Not till the vengeance that is coming comes.
For shall all hear the voice excepting God,
Or God not listen, hearing?—Lord, how long?

EMIGRATION.

WEAVE o'er the world your weft, yea weave your selves,
Imperial races, weave the warp thereof.
Swift like your shuttle speed the ships, and scoff
At wind and wave. And, as a miner delves
For hidden treasure bedded deep in stone,
So seek ye and find the treasure patriotism
In lands remote and dipped with alien chrism,
And make those new lands heart-dear and your own.
Weave o'er the world your selves. Half-human man
Wanes from before your faces like a cloud
Sun-stricken, and his soil becomes his shroud.
But of your souls and bodies ye shall make
The sovereign vesture of its leagueless span,
Clothing with history cliff and wild and lake.

HAVE no wealth of grief; no sobs, no tears,
  Not any sighs, no words, no overflow
  Nor storms of passion; no reliefs; yet oh!
I have a leaden grief, and with it fears
Lest they who think there 's nought where nought appears
  May say I never loved him. Ah, not so!
  Love for him fills my heart; if grief is slow
In utterance, remember that for years
Love was a habit and the grief is new,
  So new a thing it has no language yet.
  Tears crowd my heart: with eyes that are not wet
I watch the rain-drops, silent, large, and few,
  Blotting a stone; then, comforted, I take
  Those drops to be my tears, shed for his sake.

DAYBREAK IN FEBRUARY.

OVER the ground white snow, and in the air
Silence. The stars like lamps soon to expire,
Gleam tremblingly ; serene and heavenly fair,
The eastern hanging crescent climbeth higher.
See, purple on the azure softly steals,
And Morning, faintly touched with quivering fire,
Leans on the frosty summits of the hills,
Like a young girl over her hoary sire.
Oh, such a dawning over me has come,—
The daybreak of thy purity and love ;—
The sadness of the never-satiate tomb
Thy countenance hath power to remove ;
And from the sepulchre of Hope thy palm
Can roll the stone, and raise her bright and calm.

THE bubble of the silver-springing waves,
Castalian music, and that flattering sound,
Low rustling of the loved Apollian leaves,
With which my youthful hair was to be crowned,
Grow dimmer in my ears ; while Beauty grieves
Over her votary, less frequent found ;
And, not untouched by storms, my lifeboat heaves
Through the splashed ocean-waters, outward bound.
And as the leaning mariner, his hand
Clasped on his ear, strives trembling to reclaim
Some loved lost echo from the fleeting strand,
So lean I back to the poetic land ;
And in my heart a sound, a voice, a name
Hangs, as above the lamp hangs the expiring flame.

THE ARMY SURGEON.

OVER that breathing waste of friends and foes,
The wounded and the dying, hour by hour,
In will a thousand, yet but one in power,
He labours through the red and groaning day.
The fearful moorland where the myriads lay
Moved as a moving field of mangled worms.
And as a raw brood, orphaned in the storms,
Thrust up their heads if the wind bend a spray
Above them, but when the bare branch performs
No sweet paternal office, sink away
With helpless chirp of woe,—so, as he goes,
Around his feet in clamorous agony
They rise and fall; and all the seething plain
Bubbles a cauldron vast of many-coloured pain.

THE COMMON GRAVE.

LAST night beneath the foreign stars I stood,
And saw the thoughts of those at home go by
To the great grave upon the hill of blood.
Upon the darkness they went visibly,
Each in the vesture of its own distress.
Among them there came One, frail as a sigh,
And like a creature of the wilderness
Dug with her bleeding hands. She neither cried
Nor wept; nor did she see the many stark
And dead that lay unburied at her side.
All night she toiled; and at that time of dawn,
When Day and Night do change their More and Less,
And Day is More, I saw the melting Dark
Stir to the last, and knew she laboured on.

THE HEART KNOWETH ITS OWN BITTERNESS.

WE sat together underneath a lime,
  Whose netted branches wove an emerald night;
  And in short sentences—in low and light
Whispers—recalled the stories of old time;
Until some word, I know not what, some rhyme
  Dragged out a hidden grief, that lived—in spite
  Of creeping lichen years—such years as might
Well humble all that once was thought sublime.
My grief it was, and will be: *she* but sees
  A strangeness which she cannot understand;
A nameless tower overgrown with trees;
  A heap of stones encumbering the land;
A hearth now haunted by the wintry breeze,
  Long, long ago, by love and fancy fanned.

AD MATREM.

MUSIC, and frankincense of flowers, belong
To this sweet festival of all the year.
Take, then, the latest blossom of my song,
And to Love's canticle incline thine ear.
What is it that Love chaunts? thy perfect praise.
What is it that Love prays? worthy to prove.
What is it Love desires? thy length of days.
What is it that Love asks? return of love.
Ah, what requital can Love ask more dear
Than by Love's priceless self to be repaid?
Thy liberal love, increasing year by year,
Hath granted more than all my heart hath prayed,
And, prodigal as Nature, makes me pine
To think how poor my love compared with thine!

TO ENGLAND.

LEAR and Cordelia! 'twas an ancient tale
  Before thy Shakspeare gave it deathless fame:
  The times have changed, the moral is the same.
So like an outcast dowerless and pale,
Thy daughter went, and in a foreign gale
  Spread her young banner, till its sway became
  A wonder to the nations. Days of shame
Are close upon thee: prophets raise their wail.
When the rude Cossack with an outstretched hand
  Points his long spear across the narrow sea,—
  'Lo, there is England!' when thy destiny
Storms on thy straw-crowned head, and thou dost stand
Weak, helpless, mad, a by-word in the land,—
  God grant thy daughter a Cordelia be!

BEAUTY still walketh on the earth and air:
Our present sunsets are as rich in gold
As ere the Iliad's music was out-rolled,
The roses of the Spring are ever fair,
'Mong branches green still ring-doves coo and pair,
And the deep sea still foams its music old;
So, if we are at all divinely souled,
This beauty will unloose our bonds of care.
'Tis pleasant, when blue skies are o'er us bending
Within old starry-gated Poesy,
To meet a soul set to no worldly tune,
Like thine, sweet Friend! Oh, dearer this to me
Than are the dewy trees, the sun, the moon,
Or noble music with a golden ending.

REST.

EARTH, lie heavily upon her eyes;
Seal her sweet eyes weary of watching, Earth;
Lie close around her; leave no room for mirth
With its harsh laughter, nor for sound of sighs.
She hath no questions, she hath no replies,
Hushed in and curtained with a blessèd dearth
Of all that irked her from the hour of birth;
With stillness that is almost Paradise.
Darkness more clear than noonday holdeth her,
Silence more musical than any song;
Even her very heart has ceased to stir:
Until the morning of Eternity
Her rest shall not begin nor end, but be;
And when she wakes she will not think it long.

AFTER DEATH.

THE curtains were half drawn, the floor was swept
And strewn with rushes, rosemary and may
Lay thick upon the bed on which I lay,
Where through the lattice ivy-shadows crept.
He leaned above me, thinking that I slept
And could not hear him; but I heard him say:
'Poor child, poor child:' and as he turned away
Came a deep silence, and I knew he wept.
He did not touch the shroud, or raise the fold
That hid my face, or take my hand in his,
Or ruffle the smooth pillows for my head:
He did not love me living; but once dead
He pitied me; and very sweet it is
To know he still is warm though I am cold.

Amor, che ne la mente mi ragiona.—DANTE.
Amor vien nel bel viso di costei.—PETRARCA.

F there be any one can take my place
And make you happy whom I grieve to grieve,
Think not that I can grudge it, but believe
I do commend you to that nobler grace,
That readier wit than mine, that sweeter face;
Yea, since your riches make me rich, conceive
I too am crowned, while bridal crowns I weave,
And thread the bridal dance with jocund pace.
For if I did not love you, it might be
That I should grudge you some one dear delight;
But since the heart is yours that was mine own,
Your pleasure is my pleasure, right my right,
Your honourable freedom makes me free
And you companioned I am not alone.

AFTER COMMUNION.

HY should I call Thee Lord, who art my God?
Why should I call Thee Friend, who art my Love?
Or King, who art my very Spouse above?
Or call Thy Sceptre on my heart Thy rod?
Lo, now Thy banner over me is love,
All heaven flies open to me at Thy nod:
For Thou hast lit Thy flame in me a clod,
Made me a nest for dwelling of Thy Dove.
What wilt Thou call me in our home above,
Who now hast called me friend? how will it be
When Thou for good wine settest forth the best?
Now Thou dost bid me come and sup with Thee,
Now Thou dost make me lean upon Thy breast:
How will it be with me in time of love?

TO-DAY'S BURDEN.

'ARISE, depart, for this is not your rest.'—
Oh burden of all burdens, still to arise
And still depart, nor rest in any wise!
Rolling, still rolling thus to east from west
Earth journeys on her immemorial quest,
Whom a moon chases in no different guise.
Thus stars pursue their courses, and thus flies
The sun, and thus all creatures manifest
Unrest the common heritage, the ban
Flung broadcast on all human kind, on all
Who live; for living, all are bound to die:
That which is old, we know that it is man:
These have no rest who sit and dream and sigh,
Nor have those rest who wrestle and who fall.

DANTE.

THINK the great God gave thee unto men
To be to them what Maro was to thee—
Another gracious Beatrice to be—
Piloting souls; recording with thy pen
Things strange, and never dreamed of until then,
With coasts and islands in the Future's sea
Mapped in the clear dim light of mystery.
Preacher of Retribution! shall I, when
The bodies of the glorious dead arise
And in the Holy City re-appear
To many, find that grace to recognise
One who has led me spell-bound far and near
Through Purgatory, Hell, and Paradise,
And hail thee as earth's greatest poet-seer!

PUBLIC OPINION.

IF Conscience be the regent of man's soul,
Whose thoughts and wills are but her ministers,
Needs must she disallow the enforced control
Of thoughts she thinks not, and of wills not hers.
This Soul-made Conscience is a Queen whose cold
Strict sceptre rules her hidden realm, alone;
That Crowd-made Conscience is a harlot bold
That, owned by many, yet is no man's own;
This Conscience is responsible for one;
That Conscience irresponsible for any;
Wrong done by all men is the deed of none;
That's no man's virtue which is made by many:
Since, therefore, God no Corporate Soul hath made,
How shall this Corporate Conscience be obeyed?

THE TRIUMPH OF LOVE.

AH Love, dear Love. In vain I scoff. In vain
I ply my barren wit, and jest at thee.
Thou heedest not, or dost forgive the pain,
And in thy own good time and thy own way,
Waiting my silence, thou dost vanquish me.
Thou comest at thy will in sun or rain
And at the hour appointed, a spring day,
An autumn night—and lo, I serve again.
Forgive me, touch me, chide me. What to thee,
God that thou art, are these vain shifts of mine?
Let me but know thee. Thou alone art wise.
I ask not to be wise or great or free
Or aught but at thy knees and wholly thine,
Thus, and to feel thy hand upon mine eyes.

THE SWALLOW.

HAD I, my love declared, the tireless wing
That wafts the swallow to her northern skies,
I would not, sheer within the rich surprise
Of full-blown Summer, like the swallow, fling
My coyer being; but would follow Spring,
Melodious consort, as she daily flies,
Apace with suns, that o'er new woodlands rise
Each morn—with rains her gentler stages bring.
My pinions should beat music with her own;
Her smiles and odours should delight me ever,
Gliding, with measured progress, from the zone
Where golden seas receive the mighty river,
Unto yon lichened cliffs, whose ridges sever
Our Norseland from the Arctic surge's moan.

PERISHED IDEALS.

PASSING through life, we hold dead memories
Of aspirations which we breathe no more:
The names of masters whom we did adore
Abide with us, and at some chance may rise
And flame before us, bright as heretofore.
The transient joy we feel: but what the woe,
If that which wakened should requench the glow,
Being not what it was, but in the throng
Of dead things to be numbered now, for spent,
Save for our own heart's chance-awakened core,
Its old dominion? Thus, in Dante's song,
Pale Statius meeting Virgil would have bent
To embrace his feet: 'Nay, brother,' Virgil said,
'Thou art a shadow, and thou seest a shade.'

IVE me the darkest corner of a cloud,
  Placed high upon some lonely mountain's head,
Craggy and harsh with ruin; let me shroud
  My life in horror, for I wish me dead.
No gentle lowland known and loved of old,
  Lure me to life back through the gate of tears;
But long time drenched with rain and numb with cold,
  May I forget the solace of the years:
No trees by streams, no light and warmth of day,
  No white clouds pausing o'er the happy town;
But wind and rain, and fogbanks slow and gray,
  And stony wastes, and uplands scalped and brown;
No life, but only death in life: a grave
As cold and bleak as thine, dear soul, I crave.

HUMANITY.

THERE is a soul above the soul of each,
A mightier soul, which yet to each belongs:
There is a sound made of all human speech,
And numerous as the concourse of all songs:
And in that soul lives each, in each that soul,
Though all the ages are its lifetime vast;
Each soul that dies, in its most sacred whole
Receiveth life that shall for ever last.
And thus for ever with a wider span
Humanity o'erarches time and death;
Man can elect the universal man,
And live in life that ends not with his breath:
And gather glory that increaseth still
Till Time his glass with Death's last dust shall fill.

STRIVING to sing glad songs, I but attain
Wild discords sadder than Grief's saddest tune;
As if an owl with his harsh screech should strain
To overgratulate a thrush of June.
The nightingale upon its thorny spray
Finds inspiration in the sullen dark;
The kindling dawn, the world-wide joyous day
Are inspiration to the soaring lark;
The seas are silent in the sunny calm,
Their anthem-surges in the tempest boom;
The skies outroll no solemn thunder-psalm
Till they have clothed themselves with clouds of gloom:
My mirth can laugh and talk, but cannot sing;
My grief finds harmonies in every thing.

WOMEN WHO BLESS AND ARE BLESSED.

WHEN too, too conscious of its solitude,
My heart plains weakly as a widowed dove,
The forms of certain women sweet and good,
Whom I have known and love with reverent love,
Rise up before me; then my heart grows great
With tearful gratitude, and no more pines.
You lovely souls that fitly consecrate
The whiteness of your alabaster shrines!
You tender lives of purest good that leaven
The monstrous evils of our mortal birth!
There are no female angels up in Heaven
Because they all are women here on earth:
As once God's sons, God's daughters now come down;
But these to share, not lose, the Heavenly crown.

1862.

TO LONGFELLOW IN ENGLAND, 1868.

N English greeting to the Bard, who bears
His chaplet of sweet song from that far West
Where pine woods, with their branches low depressed,
Cease not lamenting to the scented airs,—
For Hiawatha, as he disappears,
Swift sailing to the Island of the Blest,—
And for Evangeline, who, now at rest,
With our own Gertrude's self the amaranth shares.—
Glad greeting! for, in many an English home,
The poet's voice has pierced the silent night
With chants of high Resolve, and Joys that come
At Duty's summons; then, Hope's answering light,—
Clear as the red star watching o'er the earth,—
Has glowed afresh on life's rekindled hearth.

GARIBALDI'S RETIREMENT.

NOT that three armies thou did'st overthrow;
Not that three cities oped their gates to thee,
I praise thee, Chief; not for *this* royalty
Decked with new crowns, *that* utterly laid low;
For nothing of all thou did'st forsake, to go
And tend thy vines amid the Etrurian Sea;
Not even that thou did'st *this*—though History
Retread two thousand selfish years to show
Another Cincinnatus! Rather for this,
The having lived such life, that even this deed
Of stress heroic natural seems as is
Calm night, when glorious day it doth succeed;
And we, forewarned by surest auguries,
The amazing act with no amazement read.

WILL not rail, or grieve when torpid eld
Frosts the slow-journeying blood, for I shall see
The lovelier leaves hang yellow on the tree,
The nimbler brooks in icy fetters held.
Methinks the aged eye that first beheld
The fitful ravage of December wild,
Then knew himself indeed dear Nature's child,
Seeing the common doom, that all compelled.
No kindred we to her belovèd broods
If, dying these, we drew a selfish breath;
But one path travel all her multitudes,
And none dispute the solemn Voice that saith:
'Sun to thy setting, to your autumn, woods,
Stream to thy sea, and man unto thy death!'

MOTION OF THE MISTS.

HERE by the sunless Lake there is no air,
Yet with how ceaseless motion, like a shower
Flowing and fading, do the high Mists lower
Amid the gorges of the Mountains bare.
Some weary breathing never ceases there,—
The barren peaks can feel it hour by hour;
The purple depths are darkened by its power;
A soundless breath, a trouble all things share
That feel it come and go. See! onward swim
The ghostly Mists, from silent land to land,
From gulf to gulf; now the whole air grows dim—
Like living men, darkling a space, they stand,
But lo! a Sunbeam, like the Cherubim,
Scatters them onward with a flaming brand.

SLEEP.

WHEN to soft Sleep we give ourselves away,
And in a dream as in a fairy bark
Drift on and on through the enchanted dark
To purple daybreak—little thought we pay
To that sweet bitter world we know by day.
We are clean quit of it, as is a lark
So high in heaven no human eye may mark
The thin swift pinion cleaving through the gray.
Till we awake ill fate can do no ill,
The resting heart shall not take up again
The heavy load that yet must make it bleed;
For this brief space the loud world's voice is still,
No faintest echo of it brings us pain.
How will it be when we shall sleep indeed?

COR CORDIUM.

HEART of hearts, the chalice of love's fire,
Hid round with flowers and all the bounty of bloom;
O wonderful and perfect heart, for whom
The lyrist liberty made life a lyre;
O heavenly heart, at whose most dear desire
Dead love, living and singing, cleft his tomb,
And with him risen and regent in death's room
All day thy choral pulses rang full choir;
O heart whose beating blood was running song,
O sole thing sweeter than thine own songs were,
Help us for thy free love's sake to be free,
True for thy truth's sake, for thy strength's sake strong,
Till very liberty make clean and fair
The nursing earth as the sepulchral sea.

ARMAND BARBÈS.

(1)

FIRE out of heaven, a flower of perfect fire,
That where the roots of life are had its root
And where the fruits of time are brought forth fruit;
A faith made flesh, a visible desire,
That heard the yet unbreathing years respire
And speech break forth of centuries that sit mute
Beyond all feebler footprint of pursuit;
That touched the highest of hope, and went up higher;
A heart love-wounded whereto love was law,
A soul reproachless without fear or flaw,
A shining spirit without shadow of shame,
A memory made of all men's love and awe;
Being disembodied, so be thou the same,
What need, O soul, to sign thee with thy name?

(II)

ALL woes of all men sat upon thy soul
And all their wrongs were heavy on thy head;
With all their wounds thy heart was pierced and bled.
And in thy spirit as in a mourning scroll
The world's huge sorrows were inscribed by roll,
All theirs on earth who serve and faint for bread,
All banished men's, all theirs in prison dead,
Thy love had heart and sword-hand for the whole.
'This was my day of glory,' didst thou say,
When by the scaffold thou hadst hope to climb;
For thy faith's sake, they brought thee respite; 'Nay,
I shall not die then, I have missed my day.'
O hero, O our help, O head sublime,
Thy day shall be commensurate with time.

AFTER LOOKING INTO CARLYLE'S *REMINISCENCES.*

(1)

THREE men lived yet while this dead man was young
Whose names and words endure for ever: one
Whose eyes grew dim with straining toward the sun,
And his wings weakened, and his angel's tongue
Lost half the sweetest song was ever sung,
But like the strain half uttered earth hears none,
Nor shall man hear till all men's songs are done:
One whose clear spirit like an eagle hung
Between the mountains hallowed by his love
And the sky stainless as his soul above:
And one the sweetest heart that ever spake
The brightest words wherein sweet wisdom smiled.
These deathless names by this dead snake defiled
Bid memory spit upon him for their sake.

(11)

SWEET heart, forgive me for thine own sweet sake,
Whose breath blew music once through reeds of Cam,[1]
And for my love's sake, powerless as I am
For love to praise thee, or like thee to make
Music of mirth where hearts less pure would break,
Less pure than thine, our life-unspotted Lamb.
Things hatefullest thou hadst not heart to damn,
Nor wouldst have set thine heel on this dead snake.
Let worms consume its memory with its tongue,
The pang that stabbed fair Truth, the lip that stung
Men's memories uncorroded with its breath.
Forgive me, that with bitter words like his
I mix the gentlest English name that is,
The tenderest held of all that know not death.

[1] See Charles Lamb's Sonnet written at Cambridge.

THOMAS CARLYLE.

SIRIUS has ceased from out our firmament:
Of that proud star bereft, we grope our way
Through darker nights and dawns more dull and grey.
Mentor and master! Meteor spirit, blent
Of tears and battle music; passion-rent,
Yet, crowned by years, a lamp of constant ray
To shipwrecked hearts and weary souls astray;
To what far isles is now thy message sent?
Cassandra prophet, cleaving through the cloud
With iron scourge of coward compromise,
Thou stood'st on Sinai's heights, to call aloud
Lightning and doom on all the world of lies.
Herculean Hydra-slayer; all thy days
Are gathered in a sunset storm of praise.

SWEET Mavis! at this cool delicious hour
Of gloaming, when a pensive quietness
Hushes the odorous air,—with what a power
Of impulse unsubdued dost thou express
Thyself a spirit! While the silver dew
Holy as manna on the meadow falls,
Thy song's impassioned clarity, trembling through
This omnipresent stillness, disenthrals
The soul to adoration. First I heard
A low thick lubric gurgle, soft as love,
Yet sad as memory, through the silence poured
Like starlight. But the mood intenser grows,
Precipitate rapture quickens, move on move
Lucidly linked together, till the close.

THE USE OF ANGUISH.

HE that hath once in heart and soul and sense
Absorbed the bitter juice of love that yearns
With incommunicable violence,
Still, though his love be dead and buried, burns:
Yea, if he feed not the remorseless flame
With fuel of strong thoughts for ever fresh,
The slow fire shrouded in a veil of shame
Corrodes his very substance, marrow and flesh.
Therefore in time take heed: of misery
Make wings for soaring o'er the source of pain:
Compel thy spirit's strife to strengthen thee:
And seek heaven's stars upon the hurricane
Of passionate anguish, that beyond control,
Pent in thy breast, would rack and rend thy soul.

TO THE GENIUS OF ETERNAL SLUMBER.

SLEEP, that art named eternal! Is there then
No chance of waking in thy noiseless realm?
Come there no fretful dreams to overwhelm
The feverish spirits of o'erlaboured men?
Shall conscience sleep where thou art; and shall pain
Lie folded with tired arms around her head;
And memory be stretched upon a bed
Of ease, whence she shall never rise again?
O sleep, that art eternal! Say, shall Love
Breathe like an infant slumbering at thy breast?
Shall hope there cease to throb; and shall the smart
Of things impossible at length find rest?
Thou answerest not. The poppy-heads above
Thy calm brows sleep. How cold, how still thou art!

THE VICTOR.

SOUL, rule thy self. On passion, deed, desire,
Lay thou the laws of thy deliberate will.
Stand at thy chosen post, faith's sentinel,
Though hell's lost legions ring thee round with fire.
Learn to endure. Dark vigil hours shall tire
Thy wakeful eyes; regrets thy bosom thrill;
Slow years thy loveless flower of youth may kill,
Yea, thou shalt yearn for lute and wanton lyre.
Yet is thy guerdon great: thine the reward
Of those elect who, scorning Circe's lure,
Grown early wise, make living right their lord.
Clothed with celestial steel, these walk secure;
Masters, not slaves. Over their heads the pure
Heavens bow, and guardian seraphs wave God's sword.

GOLDEN MOMENTS.

WHEN sweetest moods with fairest prospects meet,
And busy Fancy decks the world with flowers
Plucked in a land untinged by cares of ours,
Where souls, like childhood's angels, smile and greet ;
And blessèd sunshine feeds, with tempered heat,
From open skies, new blossoms through the bowers
Touched by the spirit's glory ; whilst the Hours
Their airy dance with joyous footsteps beat ;
And all the good of life seems crowded in
A few short moments :—take them unto thee ;
Drink deeply ; grasp them closely ; hide them where
Thy being flows ; for they may have to win
A little gleam through days of gloom, and be
The clearest stars that light long nights of care.

THE STRICKEN DEER.

'TIS said, that if a stag with bleeding wound
  Return to where his first companions feed,
  They have no pity for him in his need;
But turn with cruel horns, and gore him round.
So with the darkened spirit, I have found,
  Whom weight of care should to his fellows lead:
  They cry, 'This man has lost all grace indeed,
Or never had it;'—closed in self and bound:
Nor see that God's vast love and wisdom meet
  Beyond the limits of their narrow way:
That purest gold is fined by fiercest heat:
  And cloudy mornings oft make clearest day:
With hardest strokes the firmest steel is beat:
  And strongest vessel formed of well-trod clay.

FORESHADOWINGS.

(THE STARS IN THE RIVER.)

THE mirrored stars lit all the bulrush spears
And all the flags and broad-leaved lily-isles;
The ripples shook the stars to golden smiles
Then smoothed them back to happy golden spheres.
We rowed—we sang; her voice seemed, in mine ears,
An angel's, yet with woman's dearest wiles;
But shadows fell from gathering cloudy piles
And ripples shook the stars to fiery tears.

God shaped the shadows like a phantom boat
Where sate her soul and mine in Doom's attire;
Along the lily-isles I saw it float
Where ripples shook the stars to symbols dire;
We dropped the oars: I kissed her warm white throat,
While ripples shook the stars to a snake of fire.

ON THE MOUNTAINS.

(1)

NATURA BENIGNA.

WHAT power is this? What witchery wins my
feet
To peaks so sheer they scorn the cloaking snow,
All silent as the emerald gulfs below,
Down whose ice-walls the wings of twilight beat?
What thrill of earth and heaven—most wild, most sweet—
What answering pulse the guardian senses know,
Comes leaping from the ruddy eastern glow
Where, far away, the skies and mountains meet?

Mother, 'tis I once more: I know thee well,
Yet thy voice comes, an ever-new surprise!
O Mother and Queen, beneath the olden spell
Of silence, gazing from thy hills and skies!
Dumb Mother, struggling with the Years to tell
The secret at thy heart through helpless eyes!

ON THE MOUNTAINS.

(II)

NATURA MALIGNA.

THE Lady of the Hills with crimes untold
  Followed my feet, with azure eyes of prey;
  By glacier-brink she stood,—by cataract-spray,—
When mists were dire, or avalanche-echoes rolled.
At night she glimmered in the death-wind cold,
  And if a footprint shone at break of day,
  My flesh would quail, but straight my soul would say:
'Tis hers whose hand God's mightier hand doth hold.

I trod her snow-bridge, for the moon was bright,
  Her icicle-arch across the sheer crevasse,
  When lo, she stood! God bade her let me pass;
Then fell the bridge; and, in the sallow light
Adown the chasm, I saw her, cruel-white,
  And all my wondrous days as in a glass.

PARABLE SONNETS.

[Among the Bedouins a father in enumerating his children never counts his daughters, for a daughter is considered a disgrace.]

(1)

ILYÀS the prophet, lingering 'neath the moon,
  Heard from a tent a child's heart-withering wail,
  Mixt with the sorrow of the nightingale,
And, entering, found, sunk in mysterious swoon,
A little maiden dreaming there alone :—
  She babbled of her father sitting pale
  'Neath wings of Death—'mid sights of sorrow and bale—
And pleaded for his life in piteous tone.

'Poor child, plead on,' the succouring prophet saith,
  While she, with eager lips, like one who tries
  To kiss a dream, stretches her arms and cries
To Heaven for help—'Plead on; such pure love-breath,
Reaching the Throne, might stay the wings of Death
  That, in the Desert, fan thy father's eyes.'

(II)

THE drouth-slain camels lie on every hand;
Seven sons await the morning vultures' claws;
'Mid empty water-skins and camel-maws
The father sits, the last of all the band.
He mutters, drowsing o'er the moonlit sand,
'Sleep fans my brow: "Sleep makes us all pashas";[1]
Or, if the wings are Death's, why Azraeel draws
A childless father from an empty land.'

'Nay,' saith a Voice, 'the wind of Azraeel's wings
A child's sweet breath hath stilled; so God decrees':—
A camel's bell comes tinkling on the breeze,
Filling the Bedouin's brain with bubble of springs
And scents of flowers and shadow of wavering trees
Where, from a tent, a little maiden sings.

[1] Bedouin proverbial saying.

TO ALFRED TENNYSON.

(On his publishing, in his seventy-first year, the most richly-various volume of English verse that has appeared in his own century.)

BEYOND the peaks of Káf a rivulet springs
  Whose magic waters to a flood expand,
  Distilling, for all drinkers on each hand,
The immortal sweets enveiled in mortal things.
From honeyed flowers,—from balm of zephyr-wings,—
  From fiery blood of gems,[1] through all the land,
  The river draws ;—then, in one rainbow-band,
Ten leagues of nectar o'er the ocean flings.

Steeped in the riches of a poet's years,
  Stained in all colours of Man's destiny,
So Tennyson, thy widening river nears
  The misty main, and, taking now the sea,
Makes rich and warm with human smiles and tears
  The ashen billows of Eternity.

[1] According to a Mohammedan tradition, the mountains of Káf are entirely composed of gems, whose reflected splendours colour the sky.

FAITH IN DOUBT.

SOUGHT to keep the way of life—'twas hard;
Beneath me yawned the darkness, wide and deep,
I saw the blinding mists around me sweep,
And spectral forms of fear the pathway barred,
My footsteps to bewilder and retard.
No help was left, save on my knees to creep
Close to the crumbling edge, and cling and weep,
With weary limbs, and hands all bruised and scarred.

For this, methought, was faith—with desperate trust
To grasp the worn-out relics of a creed.
Beneath the strain they shivered into dust;
I reeled and fell—oh, where?—upon the breast
Of Love divine, and there, at peace indeed,
My soul in heavenly darkness lies at rest.

JACOB AND THE ANGEL.

SHALL he not bless me? will he never speak
Those words of proud concession, 'Let me go:
For the day breaketh!' Wearily and slow
The shrouded hours troop past across the peak,
Eastering; and I, with hands grown all too weak
And strength that would have failed me long ago,
But for the set soul, strain to overthrow
The instant God.—Alas! 'tis I that speak—
Not Jacob—I that in this night of days
Do wrestle with the angel Art, till breath
And gladness fail me! Yet the stern soul stays
And will not loose him till he bless me—ay,
Even though the night defer my victory
Until the day break on the dawn of death.

SIBYL.

THIS is the glamour of the world antique;
The thyme-scents of Hymettus fill the air,
And in the grass narcissus-cups are fair.
The full brook wanders through the ferns to seek
The amber haunts of bees; and on the peak
Of the soft hill, against the gold-marged sky,
She stands, a dream from out the days gone by.
Entreat her not. Indeed, she will not speak!
Her eyes are full of dreams; and in her ears
There is the rustle of immortal wings;
And ever and anon the slow breeze bears
The mystic murmur of the songs she sings.
Entreat her not: she sees thee not, nor hears
Aught but the sights and sounds of bygone springs.

SALOME.

(A PICTURE BY HENRI REGNAULT.)

FAIR sword of doom, and dripped with martyr blood
Thee Regnault saw not, whom these eyes have seen.
No Judith of the Faubourg, mænad-queen
Pale on her tumbrel-throne, when the live flood
Foams through revolted Paris, unwithstood,
Is of thy kin. Blossom and bud between,
Clear-browed Salome, with her silk head's sheen,
Lips where a linnet might have pecked at food,
Pure curves of neck, and dimpling hand aloft,
Moved like a wave at sunrise. Herod said—
'A boon for maiden freshness! ask of me
What toy may please, though half my Galilee;'
And with beseeching eyes and bird-speech soft
She fluted, 'Give me here John Baptist's head.'

THE DIVINING ROD.

HERE some time flowed my springs, and sent a cry
Of joy before them up the shining air,
While morn was new and heaven all blue and bare;
Here dipped the swallow to a tenderer sky,
And o'er my flowers rose some pure mystery
Of liquid eyes and dusky-glimmering hair;
For which lo! now, drought, death, a bright despair,
Shards, choking slag, the world's dust small and dry.
Yet turn not hence thy faithful foot, O thou,
Diviner of my buried life; pace round
Poising the hazel-rod; not all too late
The time, sweet pitier; haply, even now
Stirrings and murmurings of the underground
Prelude the flash and outbreak of my fate.

SEEKING GOD.

SAID, 'I will find God,' and forth I went
To seek Him in the clearness of the sky.
But over me stood unendurably
Only a pitiless, sapphire firmament
Ringing the world,—blank splendour; yet intent
Still to find God, 'I will go seek,' said I,
'His way upon the waters,' and drew nigh
An ocean marge weed-strewn and foam besprent;
And the waves dashed on idle sand and stone,
And very vacant was the long, blue sea;
But in the evening as I sat alone,
My window opening to the vanishing day,
Dear God! I could not choose but kneel and pray,
And it sufficed that I was found of Thee.

DON QUIXOTE.

BEHIND thy pasteboard, on thy battered hack,
  Thy lean cheek striped with plaster to and fro,
  Thy long spear levelled at the unseen foe,
And doubtful Sancho trudging at thy back,
Thou wert a figure strange enough, good lack!
  To make Wiseacredom, both high and low,
  Rub purblind eyes, and (having watched thee go)
Dispatch its Dogberrys upon thy track:
Alas! poor Knight! Alas! poor soul possest!
  Yet would to-day, when Courtesy grows chill,
And life's fine loyalties are turned to jest,
  Some fire of thine might burn within us still!
Ah, would but one might lay his lance in rest,
  And charge in earnest—were it but a mill!

Written at the time of the Bulgarian massacre, when England was on the point of lending armed support to the Turk against Russia.

(1)

STAIN not thy soul with the unholy strife,
England, my country! hear the mothers wail
At loathsome knees of murderers, whose knife
Will be less cruel to their children pale
Than those embraces with pollution rife!
Their innocents for whom they long to trail
Themselves through hells of horrible infamy!
In calm sweet homes men madden; their wild eye
Scowls on the bloody shroud that veils their life!
They curse the Tyrant, who misrules the world,
Sobbing above their darlings turned to stone;
'O strong Deliverer, who of old hast hurled
The oppressor low, arise Thou, powerful one!'
She thrusts them back: her music is their moan!

(11)

WILT thou arouse thee from low lethargy,
Only to hurl these helpless lambs to slaughter,
And fouler outrage? Souls who appeal to thee!
Therefore the Lord to blood shall change thy water,
Sea queen! for scorn named mother of the free!
Therefore innumerable ghostly laughter
Shall peal above thy vaunted empire's tomb,
What time thy pride is gathered to the gloom
Of dissolution! all shall point with glee
To the dead corse of thy colossal strength,
'There lies she who, for power and for gold,
Betrayed the innocent! laid low at length,
Who once to right the wrong towered grandly bold,
Liberty's own impregnable stronghold!'

BY THE SEA.

AH! wherefore do I haunt the shadowy tomb,
My joyless days and nights among the dead?
Know ye not he, my radiant Sun who fled,
With faint surmise consoles yon awful gloom,
Afar, upon the weltering sea's wan lead?
Behold a tremulous, ghostly gold illume
That unrevealing mystery of Doom,
Ashpale, mute wastes impenetrable! one dread
O'erwhelming purple incumbent o'er the coast.
Into the Presence-Chamber of dim Death
He hath been summoned! and I hold my post
Here in the shadow, athirst for one low breath
Released from yonder! leave me! I love my Night
More than abounding pulses of your Light!

WATCHMAN, WHAT OF THE NIGHT?

AH me, I am a singer and no seer!
  I cannot pierce these gathering clouds and chill,
  I can but lift a voice too faint to fill
The darkness, or to cheat my lonely fear.
Is the night wearing? Is the morning near?
  Lives any hope of help or comfort still?
  Hath any strength of heart to scale the hill
And tell us of the signs which thence appear?

The battle is for ever; Life and Death,
  Darkness and Light, and nowhere settled peace,
But all who live must breathe unquiet breath,
  Hunger and agonise, or wholly cease;
And for the hour, the soothest watchman saith
  He knoweth not if day or night increase.

THE WINGED SOUL.

MY soul is like some cage-born bird, that hath
A restless prescience—howsoever won—
Of a broad pathway leading to the sun,
With promptings of an oft-reprovèd faith
In sun-ward yearnings. Stricken though her breast,
And faint her wing, with beating at the bars
Of sense, she looks beyond outlying stars
And only in the Infinite sees rest.

Sad soul! If ever thy desire be bent
Or broken to thy doom, and made to share
The ruminant's beatitude,—content,—
Chewing the cud of knowledge, with no care
For germs of life within; *then* will I say,
Thou art not caged, but fitly *stalled* in clay!

CLOUDS.

THE mirky clouds that with their shade o'ercast
The sunless land with gloom and dull despair,
By sweeping hurricane and purging blast
Are riven up and split to cloudlets fair;
These passing o'er the edge of evening's realm
Go on, through breadths of amber-lighted air,
To far-off lands, and with their glory whelm
The weary world in restful influence rare.

So all our stormy thoughts and gloom of mind—
The stagnant vapour of a noontide heat—
Whirled round and cleansed by healthful stir of wind
In brighter forms their darker selves repeat.
The clouds of doubt that rise in restless youth
In mellower light dissolve to restful truth.

HER BEAUTY.

I KNEW that in her beauty was the healing
  Of sorrows, and the more than earthly cure
  Of earth-begotten ills man may endure,
Gnawed on by cares, or blown by winds of feeling;
For in her beauty was the clear revealing
  Of Truth; and with the sight a man grew pure
  And all his life and thinking steadfast, sure,
As one before a shrine of Godhead kneeling.
But then, alas! I saw that she was made
  No whit less mortal, frail,—or she might miss
    Death,—than the summer substance of a flower;
That on her beauty Death had even laid
  A touch, and in the distance called her his,
    And Time might steal her beauty every hour.

TIME'S SHADOW.

THY life, O Man, in this brief moment lies:
Time's narrow bridge whereon we darkling stand,
With an infinitude on either hand
Receding luminously from our eyes.
Lo there, thy Past's forfeited Paradise
Subsideth, like some visionary strand,
While glimmering yon, the Future's promised land
Illusive, from the abyss, seems fain to rise.

This hour alone Hope's broken pledges mar,
And joy now gleams before, now in our rear,
Like mirage mocking in some waste afar
Dissolving into air as we draw near!
Beyond our steps the path is sunny-clear:
The shadow lying only where we are.

THE DEAD.

HE Dead abide with us! Though stark and cold
Earth seems to grip them, they are with us still;
They have forged our chains of being for good or ill;
And their invisible hands these hands yet hold.
Our perishable bodies are the mould
In which their strong imperishable will—
Mortality's deep yearning to fulfil—
Hath grown incorporate through dim time untold.

Vibrations infinite of life in death
As a star's travelling light survives its star!
So let us hold our lives that when we are
The fate of those who then will draw this breath,
They shall not drag us to their judgment-bar,
And curse the heritage which we bequeath.

A SUPREME HOUR.

HE bounteous summer brings to me a day
Long waited for, long known in dim, sweet dreams:
Now 'tis a dream no more, and yet it seems
As if the hour and I were far away,—
As if with soundless footfall I did stray
Through a strange land, whose sun sheds ghostly gleams
On misty hills, dusk valleys, sleeping streams,
And shapes with shadowy life, not sad nor gay.

'Tis ever thus in hours whose running sands
Each tell a joy new-born with every breath;
The full soul pants to burst its being's bands,
And so, to seize the bliss that vanisheth,
Life stands on tip-toe, and her outstretched hands
Clasp the down-reaching hands of Sleep and Death.

TRUST me in all, for all my will is thine
    To serve thee in all things most faithfully;
    Thy henchman, asking for no nobler fee
Than that same trust, which I repay with mine.
Trust me, but trust me not as aught divine;
    Trust me with eyes wide open to all ill,
    Giving thy faith, but keeping fast thy will,
Lest in one evil scheme we both combine.
Trust me as honest, knowing I am weak,
    Stronger, but yet as much in need of aid,
    Losing no step through faith, and not afraid
To say, 'We shall not find there what we seek.'
    Lean on me, love, but not so utterly
    That if I stumble, thou shouldst helpless be.

THE ODYSSEY.

S one that for a weary space has lain
Lulled by the song of Circe and her wine
In gardens near the pale of Proserpine,
Where that Ææan isle forgets the main,
And only the low lutes of love complain,
And only shadows of wan lovers pine,
As such an one were glad to know the brine
Salt on his lips, and the large air again,
So gladly, from the songs of modern speech
Men turn, and see the stars, and feel the free
Shrill wind beyond the close of heavy flowers,
And through the music of the languid hours,
They hear like ocean on a western beach
The surge and thunder of the Odyssey.

IT was the hour before the Sun divideth
The high gates of his cloudy house at last ;
I pondered o'er the dark days of the past,
And those that, darker still, the future hideth.
Then spake the voice that mocketh aye, that chideth
My inmost heart : 'Lo thy high love is cast
Away, and thy life's stream is ebbing fast
From where thy soul in barrenness abideth.'
To still that voice, to quench heart-burning fire
What stream's forgetfulness shall we desire,
What murmuring water's soothing lullaby ?
Is it the darkness of Lethean flood,
Is it the brook that in Spring's morninghood
Waters the blue-starred flower of memory ?

ENGLAND.

NGLAND of Shakspeare, Shelley, Milton, Keats,
Burns, Byron, Wordsworth, and a thousand more
Whose voices throbbed along the self-same shore
On whose sheer margent now the swift tide beats,—
As vanquished time before thy foot retreats,
Doth high desire, and hopes that flamed of yore,
Speed likewise from thee? Is thy morning o'er?
Is it evening mist that through thy meadows fleets?

Bestir thee: every nation hath its morn,
Its noon, its even, its night of slow decay;
Lo! threatening trumpets on the breeze are borne
And harsh strange jarring clangours round thee stray,
And in the strident air thy flag is torn:—
Rise! ere thy sea-kissed kingly locks turn grey.

THE BROOK RHINE.

SMALL current of the wilds afar from men,
Changing and sudden as a baby's mood;
Now a green babbling rivulet in the wood,
Now loitering broad and shallow through the glen,
Or threading 'mid the naked shoals, and then
Brattling against the stones, half mist, half flood,
Between the mountains where the storm-clouds brood;
And each change but to wake or sleep again;
Pass on, young stream, the world has need of thee:
Far hence a mighty river on its breast
Bears the deep-laden vessels to the sea;
Far hence wide waters feed the vines and corn:
Pass on, small stream, to so great purpose born,
On to the distant toil, the distant rest.

CHOOSING.

THE thrush that, yet alone, pipes for his mate
Knows she will come in time to build the nest,
Knows she 'll be she his tiny soul loves best;
'Tis love-time at the hawthorn blossom's date:
And the new flowercups bare their hearts and wait
While careless breezes bring them love for guest;
And Youth laughs ready for the glad unrest;
But Love that chooses lingers desolate.

And I, who seek, and yearn for love to stir,
And I, who seek, and cannot love but one
And have not known her being, nor can find,
I take my homeless way for sake of her;
And love-time 's here, and love-time will be done:
Birds end all singing in the autumn wind.

LIFE.

ALAS! sweet Life, that thou must fly so fast!
Is there no breathing-place for thee and me
So much we have to say and learn and see,
So late it seems since Spring's glad moments passed;
And now the leaves change colour at the blast,
And the chill mists come creeping up the lea,
While one by one friends leave me silently
For the strange rest that ends this coil at last:
With them depart the splendour and the glow,
The fervour caught from meadow, mount, and river,
The lovely light, purer than unstained snow,
That filled dear eyes and made the pulses quiver.
Ah! let me then call back the word I said,
'Tis better life should fly when friends have fled.

A DAY'S RIDE, A LIFE'S ANALOGY.

(1)

'MID tangled forest and o'er grass-plain wide,
By many a devious path and bridle way,
Through the short brightness of an Indian day
In middle winter, 'twas my lot to ride,
Skirting the round-tipped pine-clad mountain-side,
While far beyond, upon the steely blue
Horizon, half concealed and half in view,
Himâlya's peaks upreared their snow-crowned pride
In utter purity and vast repose.
I, ere the first faint flash of morning glowed
Within her Eastern chamber, took the road,
And slowly riding between day and night
I marked how, through the wan imperfect light,
Ghostlike and grey loomed the eternal snows.

(11)

O near they seemed, each crack and crevice small
Like *bas*-relief work showed, while in the light
Of ruddy morn grey changed through pink to white.
But soon the sun upclimbing flooded all
The heavens, and then a thin and misty pall
Of exhalations rose, and pale of hue
And fainter ever those far summits grew,
Until the day waned low, and shadows tall
Sloped eastward. Then once more in radiance clear
Of setting sunlight, beautiful as brief,
Each peak and crag stood out in bold relief,
Till slowly pink faded to ghostly grey :
So through life's morning, noontide, evening, may
Ideal hope dawn, fade, and reappear.

THE PIPE-PLAYER.

COOL, and palm-shaded from the torrid heat,
The young brown tenor puts his singing by,
And sets the twin pipe to his lips to try
Some air of bulrush-glooms where lovers meet;
O swart musician, time and fame are fleet,
Brief all delight, and youth's feet fain to fly!
Pipe on in peace! To-morrow must we die?
What matter, if our life to-day be sweet!
Soon, soon, the silver paper-reeds that sigh
Along the Sacred River will repeat
The echo of the dark-stoled bearers' feet,
Who carry you, with wailing, where must lie
Your swathed and withered body, by and by,
In perfumed darkness with the grains of wheat.

IMPORTUNITY.

STAND before you as a beggar stands,
Who craves an alms, and will not be denied,
Nor shall I cease to wander by your side,
Until I gain this bounty at your hands:—
Grant me your weary thoughts, your hours of pain,
Your dull grey mornings, and your hopeless moods;
If one sad memory mar your solitudes,
Give that to me, and be at ease again.
Behold, my heart is large enough to bear
Your burdens, and to rock your heart to sleep;
Give me your griefs; I do not ask to share
The golden harvest of the joys you reap;
Be glad alone; but when your soul 's opprest,
Come here and lay your head and be at rest.

A PORTRAIT.

SHE hath lived so silently and loved so much
That she is deeply stirred by little things,
While pain's long ache and sorrow's sharper stings
Scarce move her spirit that eludes their clutch;
But one half-tone of music, or the touch
Of some tame bird's eager vibrating wings,
Breaks up the sealèd fountain's murmurings
To storm, or what in others might seem such;
So, when she lifts her serious lids to turn
On ours her soft and magical dark eyes,
All womanhood seems on her, in disguise;
As on the pale white peacock we discern
The pencilled shadows of the radiant dyes
And coloured moons that on her sisters burn.

ON CERTAIN CRITICS.

THERE are who bid us chant this modern age,
With all its shifting hopes and crowded cares,
School-boards and land-laws, tithes and state-affairs,
And, one by one, the puny wars we wage;
They charge us with our lyric flutes assuage
The hunger that the lean-ribbed peasant bears,
Or wreathe our laurel round the last grey hairs
Of the old pauper in his workhouse-cage,—
Not wisely; for the round world spins so fast,
Leaps in the air, staggers, and shoots, and halts,—
We know not what is false or what is true;
But in the firm perspectives of the past
We see the picture duly, and its faults
Are softly moulded by a filmy blue.

FRIENDSHIP.

TO F. S. W.

ACROSS the vast of ocean, on the shore
  That claims you for her own by right of birth,
  Receive this echo from the older earth
Which by the right of friendship claims you more,
And by remembrance deep in the heart's core
  Of those you parted from but now, of worth
  Whose new removal makes us feel a dearth
Whereof we had not prescience before:
Yet whose insistance does but grow more strong
  And but the more enduring as the days
    Follow each other, and their spaces lend
New joy to our glad meeting in the throng
  Of hurrying men, new light to the Fate's ways
    That of a passing stranger made a friend.

LOVE AND MUSIC.

I LISTENED to the music broad and deep,
I heard the tenor in an ecstasy
Touch the sweet distant goal, I heard the cry
Of prayer and passion, and I heard the sweep
Of mighty wings, that in their going keep
The music that the spheres make endlessly;
Then my cheeks shivered, tears made blind each eye,
As flame to flame I felt the quick blood leap,
And through the tides and moonlit winds of sound
To me love's passionate voice grew audible:
Again I felt your heart to my heart bound,
Then silence on the viols and voices fell;
But, like the still, small voice within a shell,
I heard Love thrilling through the void profound.

IN EARLY SPRING.

THE delicate wind, clear light of the warm sun!
  Surely I know how subtly sweet is Spring,
  The earth and man's worn heart revisiting;
I would not have thy brief existence done.
And yet I would, Oh new-born Spring, that one
  Might meet thine eyes without there mirroring
  The ghost of many a sweet and bitter thing,
Old dreads, old hopes too frail to lean upon.

Oh last descended of a hostile race,
  Though in thyself so sweet and softly fair,
Within thine eyes ancestral springs I trace;
So some wronged woman in her baby's face
  May shuddering see its father's likeness there,
  While parted raptures thrill through her despair.

LEAST LOVE.

THIS small least love of mine, which can but creep
  Between the twisted stems of joy and pain,
  Is warmed by sun and bathed by every rain:
Last night, transplanted to the fields of sleep,
It blossomed so I could not choose but weep,
  Knowing the sweet, familiar scent again.
  Mostly it grows unnoticed, fair, and fain
In depths of sunlit air its leaves to steep;
But there are times when every fairer flower
  Looks cold, unsympathetic, in my sight;
Then am I glad to turn, in such an hour,
  To this my blossom, neither red nor white,
Holding the fragrance of the last warm shower;
  But, gather it, it fades before the night.

SPRING.

STAND as on the verge of life; 'tis Spring,
When springs are welling ere they brim away;
When waking birds just cheep and shake their wing,
And clouds come winding in the virgin day;
I look through fruit boughs fresh with sprout and spray,
Down loam-hills loose by shoots where dew-drops cling,
From out the deep sky night yet dreams away,
Down lush marsh woods and waters wandering.
I stand between the past and the pursuing,
Between the dreamed of deed and the undone,
With all the earth on tiptoe for the doing,
And breathless for the start-word of the sun;
And dreaming drifts away and big with song
My full heart fails when it should be most strong.

INTER MANES.

IN the dim watches of the midmost night
A ghost confronts him, standing by his bed,
A lonesome ghost who walks uncomforted,
Pale child of Memory and dead Delight
No longer fair or pleasant in his sight.
With dusky hair upon her shoulders shed,
And cypress leaves for garland on her head,
As patient as the moonlight and as white,
She stands beside him and puts forth her hand
To lead him backward into Love's lost Land—
Sad Land which shadows people, and where wait
Memory, her sire, and dead Delight, his mate—
And standing there among the shadowy band
He learns how Love mocks him who loves too late.

THE MARSEILLAISE.

WHAT means this mighty chant, wherein the wail
Of some intolerable woe, grown strong
With sense of more intolerable wrong,
Swells to a stern victorious march—a gale
Of vengeful wrath? What mean the faces pale,
The fierce resolve, the ecstatic pangs along
Life's fiery ways, the demon thoughts which throng
The gates of awe, when these wild notes assail
The sleeping of our souls? Hear we no more
Than the mad foam of revolution's leaven,
Than a roused people's throne-o'erwhelming tread?
Yes: 'tis man's spirit thundering on the shore
Of iron fate; the march of Titans dread,
Sworn to dethrone the gods unjust from heaven.

O more these passion-worn faces shall men's eyes
Behold in life. Death leaves no trace behind
Of their wild hate and wilder love, grown blind
With desperate longing, more than the foam which lies
Splashed up awhile where the cold spray descries
The waves whereto their cold limbs were resigned;
Yet ever doth the sea-wind's undefined
Vague wailing shudder with their dying sighs.
For all men's souls 'twixt sorrow and love are cast,
As on the earth each lingers his brief space,
While surely nightfall comes, where each man's face
In death's obliteration sinks at last
As a deserted wind-tossed sea's foam-trace—
Life's chilled boughs emptied by death's autumn-blast.

THE PAST DETHRONED.

THY reign is done. The old fresh springs are fled,
The amorous summers are burned out and cold,
Scattered and spent is autumn's ruddy gold,
And light the earth lies on fierce winter's head;
The Past, or good or ill, is done and dead,
And shall not rise: bury the corpse: behold
The Future beckons beautiful and bold,—
Bury the corpse and let no tears be shed.

'Tis in my heart as in some tyrant's court
Where men have trembled 'neath the pale King's frown
Hour after hour in silence, till kneels one
To sue for mercy at his feet,—stops short,—
Cries *He is dead* and hurls him headlong down,
And the air rings with joy. Thy reign is done.

MY HEART SHALL BE THY GARDEN.

QUESTO NE' PATTI NOSTRI, AMOR, NON ERA.
LORENZO DE' MEDICI.

Y heart shall be thy garden. Come, my own,
Into thy garden; thine be happy hours
Among my fairest thoughts, my tallest flowers,
From root to crowning petal thine alone.
Thine is the place from where the seeds are sown
Up to the sky, enclosed, with all its showers.
But ah, the birds, the birds! Who shall build bowers
To keep these thine? O friend, the birds have flown.

For as these come and go, and quit our pine
To follow the sweet season, or, new comers,
Sing one song only from our alder-trees,
My heart has thoughts, which, though thine eyes hold mine,
Flit to the silent world and other summers,
With wings that dip beyond the silver seas.

RENOUNCEMENT.

MUST not think of thee; and, tired yet strong,
I shun the love that lurks in all delight—
The love of thee—and in the blue Heaven's height,
And in the dearest passage of a song.
Oh just beyond the sweetest thoughts that throng
This breast, the thought of thee waits hidden yet bright;
But it must never, never come in sight;
I must stop short of thee the whole day long.

But when sleep comes to close each difficult day,
When night gives pause to the long watch I keep,
And all my bonds I needs must loose apart,
Must doff my will as raiment laid away,—
With the first dream that comes with the first sleep
I run, I run, I am gathered to thy heart.

SPRING WIND.

O FULL-VOICED herald of immaculate Spring,
With clarion gladness striking every tree
To answering raptures, as a resonant sea
Fills rock-bound shores with thunders echoing—
O thou, each beat of whose tempestuous wing
Shakes the long winter-sleep from hill and lea,
And rouses with loud reckless jubilant glee
The birds that have not dared as yet to sing:—

O wind, that comest with prophetic cries,
Hast thou indeed beheld the face that is
The joy of poets and the glory of birds—
Spring's face itself:—hast thou 'neath bluer skies
Met the warm lips that are the gates of bliss,
And heard June's leaf-like whisper of sweet words?

LOVER'S SILENCE.

HEN she whose love is even my air of life
Enters, delay being past, to bless my home,
And ousts her phantom from its place, being come
Herself to fill it; when the importunate strife
Of absence with desire is stilled, and rife
With heaven is earth; why am I stricken dumb,
Abashed, confounded, awed of heart and numb,
Waking no triumph of song, no welcoming fife?

Be thine own answer, soul, who long ago
Didst see the awful light of Beauty shine,
Silent; and silently rememberest yet
That glory which no spirit may forget;
Nor utter save in love a thought too fine
For souls to ignore, or mortal sense to know.

A VISION OF PAIN.

FRAUGHT with sad benediction, as the leaves
  Of night-fed Upas in the midmost climes
  Each morning's blessing may dispense betimes,—
His palsied fingers span the crowd that heaves
Beneath, and, madly restless, idly grieves
  Because its joys are lesser than its crimes ;
  His speech is rhythmic with a strange sea's chimes,
And all his tropes are soul-incantatives.
O mystery of kingship that he wears
  On throne of sacrifice, to right the wrong !
For love of him the poet takes his cares
  And with baptismal sacrament calls them song,
And yearningly saints kiss his sceptral rod,
At sight of eyes that shine like tears of God !

HISTORY.

DARKLY, as by some gloomèd mirror glassed,
Herein at times the brooding eye beholds
The great scarred visage of the pompous Past,
But oftener only the embroidered folds
And soiled regality of his rent robe,
Whose tattered skirts are ruined dynasties
And cumber with their trailing pride the globe,
And sweep the dusty ages in our eyes,
Till the world seems a world of husks and bones
Where sightless Seërs and Immortals dead,
Kings that remember not their awful thrones,
Invincible armies long since vanquishèd,
And powerless potentates and foolish sages
Lie 'mid the crumbling of the massy ages.

NOTES.

LEIGH HUNT (*Book of the Sonnet*) says, that Spenser with all his Italian proclivities was the first who deliberately abandoned the archetypal pattern of the sonnet, which Sir Thomas Wyat and the Earl of Surrey are believed to have brought back with them from Italy when (fresh from the schools of Dante, Petrarch, and Ariosto) they set themselves to the work of reforming English metre and style. It is hard to understand this statement, for Surrey, who died five years before the year of Spenser's birth, wrote in the structure adopted in the great body of Spenser's sonnets. A slight divergence of structure is indeed seen in Spenser's method of linking together the several parts of his sonnet by the repetitions of rhymes (the fifth line rhyming with the fourth, and the ninth with the eighth), but so far from indicating a deliberate abandonment of the archetypal model, this variation rather signalises a desire to return to it with a view to that rounded unity which is imperfectly felt where the three quatrains stand apart in scheme of rhyme.

Edmund Spenser
—
Pages 1-4.

'The last line of this sonnet is a little obscured by a transposition. He means, Do they call ungratefulness there a virtue?'—CHARLES LAMB.

Sir Philip Sidney
—
Page 5.

The series of sonnets, *Astrophel and Stella*, from which the above is quoted, appear to record Sidney's love for Penelope Devereux, sister to the second Earl of Essex and wife of Lord Rich. Southey, however, in a letter to Sir Egerton Brydges, says Sidney's Stella cannot have been Lady Rich, because the poems plainly relate to a successful passion, and because the name was by contemporaries applied to the widow of Sidney.

This sonnet appears in the *Arcadia* immediately after a fine passage on the condition of the soul after death, and when the two friends, Musidorus and Pyrocles, are in peril of being put to death. It may be presumed that Milton's warning in his *Eikonoklastes* against 'the vaine amatoreous Poem of Sir Philip Sidney's *Arcadia*,' which was 'not to be read at any time without good caution,' scarcely applied to this sonnet, which is indeed so full of a pious resignation as to be worthy even 'in time of trouble and affliction to be a Christian's prayer-book.' Of course Milton's strictures on the 'worth and witt' of the book in question were primarily provoked by King Charles's inopportune enjoyment of them.

'His Sonnet to Sleep became a kind of model to younger writers, and imitations of it are to be found in the sonneteers of the time, sometimes with the opening epithet literally borrowed.'—G. SAINTSBURY, *The English Poets*, vol. i.

It would be extremely difficult to prove that the opening epithet of this sonnet originated with Daniel, though Bartholomew Griffin's employment of it in his *Fidessa* is an obvious appropriation from him. It does not appear to have been observed in this connection that certain lines of Griffin's derived sonnet (published about 1596) are clearly the germ of the great passage on sleep in *Macbeth*, probably written about 1606. It need hardly be said that in this case, as in other cases of Shakspeare's apparent borrowings, the coincidences are merely verbal, and that the spirit of what is said by Griffin undergoes complete transfiguration, such as raises it to a level proper to the greater poet. Daniel appears to have been regarded with some amount of favour by his contemporaries, but subsequent critics judged him prosaic, and he was in danger of falling entirely out of sight when Coleridge, Wordsworth, and Southey, in the days of the first *Lyrical Ballads*, discovered in him excellent specimens of that neutral style which they were then asserting was common to good prose and natural verse; and henceforward these poets lost no opportunity of commending a writer who seemed to them often to write in language as easy and natural as it was pure. Another set of excellences, a richness and an occasional exuberance of epithet, attached Leigh Hunt and the London school to this chaste, amiable, and serious poet, and again the 'well-languaged Daniel' took poetic rank, to which his *Musophilus* and *Hymen's Triumph* (abounding as they nevertheless do with passages of exceptional beauty) seem scarcely to have entitled him. One later champion (in addition to his modern editor, Dr. Grosart) Daniel has indeed secured in the gifted and right-hearted William Davies, author of *Songs of a Wayfarer.* In a paper on the Sonnet published in the *Quarterly Review*, January 1873, Mr. Davies says that for mellifluous tenderness and pensive grace of expression, the above might rank amongst the first sonnets in the language.

Michael Drayton. — Page 12

There are many English sonnets treating of love-parting, and certain of the most notable of them are by Elizabethan and Victorian poets of great name, but by a general agreement of catholic opinion this is amongst all similar sonnets quite incomparable. As a piece of self-portrayal it is matchless. Those who long for something simply thought and simply said will find it charming in the full first sense of that injured word, whilst those who demand psychical insight will realise in it a profundity as deep as the whole depth of the spirit of love in humanity. Observe specially the contrast of the mock outbraving tone in the opening passages, and the strong yearning of confessed passion in the unmasked close,—now first so separated that the contrast may be the better felt. The marvel is that this sonnet stands almost alone in excellence in the works of a poet who wrote a cycle of sixty-three sonnets in all, mostly disfigured by conceits and plays upon words. Under a pseudonym Drayton completely veiled the identity of his 'Faire Idea, Soule-shrin'd Saint,' but from the sonnets themselves and from a passage in *Polyolbion*, it is supposed that she was Anne Goodeere, daughter of his patron, Sir Henry Goodeere, of Powlesworth Abbey. The lovers were finally separated, probably by difference of social position. It is curious that a recent critic speaks of Drayton as one who promised to confer an immortality upon his lady which his verse has not realised.

William Shakspeare. — Page 16.

'The trumpet-tone of all these lines is wondrously inspiriting; they express a perfect and splendid confidence. That Shakspeare, who led an inconspicuous life, and took no heed for the preservation of any of his writings later than the *Venus and Adonis* and the *Lucrece*, should yet have known with such entire certainty that they would outlive the perishing body of men and things, till the Resurrection of the Dead—this is the most moving fact in his extant history; the one which informs with grandeur of being, and reconciles into a potent unity, the residual elements of his career, sparse and disparate at best, sometimes insignificant and incongruous-looking.'—W. M. ROSSETTI, *Lives of Famous Poets.*

Page 19. It is proposed (the late Mr. Staunton, *Athenæum*, January 31, 1874) to read *crime* for *time* at the end of the sixth line. The alteration would rob the succeeding four lines of half their significance and all their relevancy. The *sweetest buds, unstained prime*, and *ambush of young days* are phrases clearly designed to emphasise the previous tribute to the purity of the author's subject; namely, that being good, slander but proves his worth the greater, because it so directs men's eyes as to compel them to see that though still of that time of life when evil woos its utmost (and when he might with least of guilt fall into vice) he is yet either not assailed by it or victor over it. Yet this praise (negative and enforced as it is) cannot tie up envy, which indeed grows the more as praise is wrung out of slander. In short, if suspicion of some ill did not attach to the subject, then he alone of all men whatever would own the universal goodwill.

Page 20. One of the least irrational and certainly one of the least harmful of the many theories which have been started by those who repudiate the simple and natural significance of Shakspeare's sonnets, is that of the late Richard Simpson, who argues that, together with the principal Elizabethan sonnet-systems, they were written in conformity with the love-philosophy of the schools, and that therefore they are not to be understood as in any sense 'accidental,' but as being written altogether passionlessly, in a *scala amoris* which demanded that all the joys and all the sorrows of love should find systematical expression. This theory is akin to that which goes to prove that the early Italian poets often used love as a metaphor where politics and scepticism were covertly involved,—and it is open to the same objection, that of robbing the poetry in question of the beauty that attaches to it from its appearance of sincerity. The known facts, however, of the amours of certain of the Elizabethan poets, seem to give colour to the rumour current amongst subsequent critics, that the agonies of unrequited affection often existed only in verse. In the case of Shakspeare's sonnets, on the other hand, the internal evidence of reality is not merely more forcible than elsewhere among the sonnets of his contemporaries, but the external evidence appears conclusive as to their having some personal application.

Page 22

The Editor has preserved the halting and puzzling punctuation of the first line observed in the original source, because the accepted reading seems to require it. The *when* in that line appears to him to present the baffling difficulty, breaking as it does the flow of the passage and the unity of thought. He suggests as a feasible emendation both of words and pointing :

'Then hate me, an' thou wilt, if ever, now.'

Precedent in abundance for such literary form will be readily remembered from Shakspeare.

Page 24

Surely it robs this sonnet of half its beauty and direct sincerity to dig beneath the surface for symbolical allusions such as appears to prove (see F. G. Fleay, *Macmillan's Magazine*, March 1875) that the absence, journey, and travel here dwelt upon do not refer to an actual journey at all, but to the separation between Southampton and Shakspeare caused by the unfaithfulness of the latter in producing not poems dedicated to his friend, but only dramas destined for the multitude. When we think how much of the above sonnet may be so strained as to seem to bear a metaphorical significance, we must needs shrink from a foreshadowing sense of how painfully that charm of simple, unaffected truthfulness which (with all the mystery of personal reference) pervades Shakspeare's sonnets must vanish beneath a touch that compels them to labour in a pregnancy of which they can never in this world be delivered.

Page 25. Mr. Gerald Massey's extraordinary 'dramatic' theory regarding the sonnets of Shakspeare appears at no point more reasonable than where he argues that the above was Shakspeare's congratulation to the Earl of Southampton on his release from the Tower on the death of Elizabeth. But our agreement with Mr. Massey is rather in default of a better explanation than because we find his view a satisfying one. The sonnet is so heavily laden with thought (especially in the opening passages), and is throughout so informed by incidents alluded to but not explained, that it may be freely admitted (the foregoing note notwithstanding) that it stands in some need of collateral explanation. One line only, the fourth, contains direct allusion to such confinement as Mr. Massey associates with it, and two only, the fifth and fourteenth, can be supposed to refer to the death of the sovereign, whilst only the word *forfeit* appears to point to a committal such as that of Southampton, which was occasioned by complicity in the Essex conspiracy. The remainder of the sonnet (four-fifths of it) may surely with equal appropriateness denote any time of rejoicing following a period of anxiety as the event with which Mr. Massey connects it. Whilst saying this, I must add that I myself think that the sonnet does certainly refer to the death of Elizabeth and accession of James, but not to the imprisonment of Southampton.

'This sonnet appears to be imitated in one by Drayton, upon the alterations made by Time "since first his love began," in which mention is made of the "quiet end of that long loving queen" and "this king's fair entrance."'—Henry Brown, *Sonnets of Shakspeare Solved.*

Perhaps the natural significance of that large part of Shakspeare's sonnets which is always (and now more than ever) in dispute lies on the surface of them in their simple record (whereof the only difficulties of interpretation come of laboured condensation of difficult thought) of the love given to a noble man by a man yet nobler—this and no more, through all the changeful moods of one whose temper was variable. If the language of affection employed between the friends appears highly coloured and exaggerated, let it be asked wherein it differs from the conversation of Musidorus and Pyrocles in the *Arcadia*.

Better guides to an unaffected reading of what is known as the Herbert series I do not know than Professor Dowden in his edition of Shakspeare's Sonnets, and Mr. W. M. Rossetti in his *Lives of Famous Poets.* The latter of these critics mentions one point (Pembroke's resemblance to his mother) which seems finally to settle the question at issue (as to the identity of Shakspeare's friend) to the satisfaction of all who refuse to believe that Thorpe could have resorted to the clumsy artifice of reversing the initials of the dedicatee in order to conceal the personality of Henry Wriothesley, without reflecting that thereby he turned the eyes of the public on Shakspeare's other patron, William Herbert, Earl of Pembroke.

It affords an agreeable and tranquilising relief to turn from some painful disputations in which (after hurling firebrands at a figure of their own imagining) critics affect regret that our great and gentle Shakspeare could have submitted himself to lawless passions, to so pure and perfect an abstraction of the spirit of love in humanity as is contained in this sonnet. Reality of chaste affection, abnegating, constant, elevating, is stamped so forcibly on every line, that it seems inconceivable that a true-hearted nature can suspect the series of which it is a part of being anywhere debased by covert touches of unhealthy sentiments. Grapes do not grow on thistles, and a thing so tender and stainless as this could not come from one whose basis of nature was other than healthy, manly, and noble. Tragedy, indeed, there may have been in Shakspeare's life, and weakness also in his nature (if we may read between the lines of the second series of sonnets, beginning with 127), but here we see with what changeless nobleness the one was met, and with what unselfish submission the other was borne. It is not a necessity incumbent upon any lover of Shakspeare to prove that the best of poets was also the best of men; but the reader of his sonnets who contents himself with their simple significance, will find it difficult to light upon any work extant which proves more conclusively from its unequalled love of human nature and superhuman insight into it (for guilt petrifies the heart whilst it beclouds the mind) that the author must have been scarcely less amiable and good than wise and great. Page 26.

'The subject, the bitter delusion of all sinful pleasures, the reaction of Page 27 a swift remorse which inevitably dogs them, Shakspeare must have most deeply felt, as he has expressed himself upon it most profoundly. I know of no picture of this at all so terrible in its truth as, in *The Rape of Lucrece*, the description of Tarquin after he has successfully wrought his deed of shame. But the sonnet on the same theme is worthy to stand by its side.'—ARCHBISHOP TRENCH, *Household Book of English Poetry*.

Page 28. This sonnet appears, with many variations upon the reading given in the text, in *The Passionate Pilgrim*.

Page 29. The quarto reads—

'My sinful earth these rebel powers that thee array.'

The correction is by Malone, amended by Dyce.

There has long been a fruitless search through Milton's *Paradise Lost* for a sonnet which Wordsworth orally declared to be discoverable somewhere in the poem. However this may be, it is an undoubted fact that the sestet of a Shakspearean sonnet has found its way into the first scene of the second Act of *Richard II.*:—

He that no more may say is listened more
  Than they whom youth and ease have taught to gloze;
More are man's ends marked than their lives before:
  The setting sun, and music at the close,
As the last taste of sweets is sweetest last,
Writ in remembrance more than things long past.

It is doubtful if anything finer appears in the whole series of the sonnets themselves.

John Donne. Page 30. The Editor has experienced some difficulty in selecting more than a single sonnet by Donne to accompany the magnificent one on Death. Concerning that masterpiece, there can hardly be a doubt that it is the weightiest, most forceful and full-thoughted of all the many English sonnets written on the subject. But Donne's other sonnet work, while distinguished by great power of fundamental conception, and (although rugged in workmanship) by occasional felicity of phrase, is throughout disfigured by metaphysical involution, and by a proneness to degenerate into a sort of metaphysical antithesis very damaging to poetic harmony. Moreover, his sonnets are frequently so linked each to each (the last line of a sonnet forming the first of its successor), that few of them are found to possess that unity of thought which would admit of each standing alone. It were scarcely accurate to say Donne is unequal, for his one great effort apart, his sonnets have very balanced merit.

William Drummond.

Pages 33-37

Drummond said that Drayton seemed rather to love his muse than his mistress, judging by his many artificial similes, which showed the quality of his mind, but not the depth of his passion. Perhaps Drummond alone of the poets of his period, excepting Shakspeare only, had just licence to write so, for what he says with truth of Drayton might with equal appropriateness have been urged against all his other contemporaries save one. A wanton desire to revel in pretty conceits at any sacrifice of naturalness and to all but total disregard of fundamental emotional prompting (which had the damaging effect of drawing off attention from the subject of a poem and centring it upon the poet) was of course the besetting weakness of the Elizabethan sonnet-writers. In Shakspeare's case the many felicitous thoughts felicitously expressed, in the poems spoken in his own person, are always subordinated to a mastering passion, which often leaves the mind too much exhausted by the emotional tension to be at once capable of realising the full splendour of the poetic medium. And Drummond also was free from excess of the kind that marred contemporaries possessed of more vital impulse ; for much that reality of absorbing passion did for Shakspeare in preserving him from the artificial expression of affected suffering, time itself acting healingly on a great sorrow did for him. After the early book in which he told the story of his life's one loss, Drummond seemed to sit above the need of that languishing craving for love-experience which was the will-o'-the-wisp which led his contemporaries into one knows not what quagmires of poetic mockery. Drummond's sonnets are wholly devoid of those excellences of conception and phrase which, where they exist in the best of his brother poets, seem to be delved out of the full depth of a deep nature, but they are distinguished by a healthful seriousness and enlarged view of life and its operative relationships, such as must have come to him equally from his patient submission to untoward circumstance, and from the distance at which he stood removed from the irritating atmosphere of small rivalries, which in London narrowed the sympathies of men so much above him in original gift as Ben Jonson.

William Browne. — Page 38. 'Browne is one of those poets whom few but children and poets will either like or love.'—HARTLEY COLERIDGE, *Essays and Marginalia*.

'There is an English poet of a later day with whom Browne may fairly be brought into some sort of comparison. That poet is Keats. It is unnecessary to say that Browne is a poet of a quite different and lower rank; but he is like Keats in being before all things an artist. * * * One thinks of Keats passing a fine phrase over his mental palate with an almost sensual pleasure. "I look upon fine phrases like a lover," he himself says in one passage; and in a lesser sense one can fancy much the same thing of Browne.'—W. T. ARNOLD, *The English Poets*, vol. ii.

In support of Mr. Arnold's speculative parallel, it will be remembered that Keats prefaced his *Epistles* with a passage from Browne's *Britannia's Pastorals*.

George Herbert. — Page 39. 'Equally admirable for the weight, number, and expression of the thoughts, and for the simple dignity of the language, unless, indeed, a fastidious taste should object to the latter half of the sixth line.'—COLERIDGE, *Biographia Literaria*.

John Milton. — Page 40. In this sonnet *Ruth* and *ruth* are made to rhyme to each other, but, as Newton observes, the old writers were not so fastidious as ourselves, and the reader may find parallel instances in Spenser's *Faery Queen*, I. vi. 39, VII. vi. 38. Shelley, Swinburne, and others, assume the same latitude.

Page 41. 'Darwen,' a river near Preston, where Cromwell routed the Scotch in 1648. This sonnet is dated May 1652, and is an appeal to Cromwell to resist the proposal to establish a paid ministry, made to him by certain Presbyterian ministers at a Committee for the Propagation of the Gospel.

On this point of policy Cromwell differed from the poet. The sonnet must have been written later than the two divorce sonnets (which appear to belong to the period of the Westminster Assembly), but it is embittered by the same hatred of the Scotch as marks the *Tetrachordon* sonnet, in which Milton endeavours to bring into contempt certain well-known Scottish surnames of an ill sound. There can be little doubt that Milton's divorce pamphlets originated in his own domestic infelicities, but a sense of personal grievance is kept entirely out of view in his treatises, wherein, indeed, the author is felt to be reasoning the question judiciously on the broadest issues, even whilst in actual fact he must have been sweltering under the full rigour of concealed passion. It was only natural that his writings should bring him under the ban of the Presbyterians, but the puritanical clutch of the Church judicatories he never wholly forgave.

The facts of the Piedmontese massacre cannot be better told than in the opening words of Cromwell's letter addressed to the Duke of Savoy, and dated May 25, 1655. Page 41.

'Letters have reached us from Geneva, and also from the Dauphinate and many other places bordering on your dominion, by which we are informed that the subjects of your Royal Highness professing the reformed religion were recently commanded by your edict and authority, within three days after the promulgation of the said edict, to depart from their habitations and properties under pain of death and forfeiture of all their estates, unless they should give security that, abandoning their own religion, they would within twenty days embrace the Roman Catholic one.'

Milton was at this time Latin Secretary Extraordinary to the Protector, and it is supposed that in that capacity he composed the Latin speech delivered by Samuel Morland, who was selected as the Protector's Commissioner to bear his letter to the Duke of Savoy.

The speech contains the following description of the massacre :—

'Houses smoking everywhere, torn limbs, the ground bloody. Ay, and virgins, ravished and hideously abused, breathed their last miserably ; and old men and persons labouring under illness were committed to the flames ; and some infants were dashed against the rocks, and the brains of others were cooked and eaten. Atrocity horrible and before unheard of, savagery such that, good God, were all the Neros of all times and ages to come to life again, what a shame they would feel at having contrived nothing equally inhuman! * * * Do not, great God, do not seek the revenge due to this iniquity!'

It can hardly be said that this is distinctly Miltonic either in spirit or style. Nor does it seem probable that Milton could be the means of putting into the mouth of a Commissioner a speech yet more audacious than the letter of the Protector. The act would have a touch of cowardice attaching to it. The utmost value that belongs to the speech arises out of the evidence it seems to afford that Milton's sonnet must have been written before Morland left England, and read and rendered by him into Latin prose. Milton would assuredly never reclothe his opening invocation as it is found in the last clause above quoted. Indeed, portions of the passage read like a prose version of the poem written by one (not a poet) for whom it had a powerful appeal.

Page 44. This sonnet was written about 1656, immediately after the death of his second wife.

Page 45. Hallam and certain other writers have declared themselves unable to reconcile their judgment to the frequent violation of the legitimate structure in Milton's sonnets. It is true that the pause between the major and minor portions of the sonnet (so uniformly observed in the best Italian examples) is not to be found in Milton, but the rhyme-scheme is always faultlessly in conformity with the most rigid rule, and the sonnets, even where they link themselves together—as in the cases of the two divorce sonnets and the two sonnets on his blindness—stand alone in self-centred unity, and never become sonnet stanzas. The serious divergence favoured by Milton in his practice of running octave into sestet was clearly the result of a deliberate conviction that the sonnet in his hands was too short a poem to be broken into halves, and hence his sonnets, each done in a breath as to metrical flow, possess the intellectual unity of oneness of conception, at the same time that they are devoid of the twofold metrical and intellectual unity which comes of the rounded perfectness of linked and contrasted parts. Much may be said for the beauty of the sonnet structure adopted by Milton, and indeed the model has been so much in requisition in recent years, that it appears to merit the distinct nomenclature which, in the index of metrical groups, I have ventured to give it. One further point (not much mentioned) is that Milton was the first great poet who gave the sonnet an objective vocation, making it a medium for political utterance, in which practice he found no great following until Wordsworth began to write in acknowledged imitation of him. It says much for the neglect into which this form of composition had fallen in the generation preceding our own, that so recently as 1853 a critic of such poetic insight as Gilfillan could find nothing more to the purpose to say of Milton's sonnets than that the subjects of them seemed always struggling to outleap their simple limits. We see now well enough that they are exactly fitted to those limits, and that they are so eminently sonnet-subjects that they could hardly exist apart from them.

This sonnet was addressed to Cyriac Skinner, one of Milton's Aldersgate Street pupils, and a member of Harrington's political club. Upon Milton's enemies imputing his blindness to the judgment of Providence upon him for his republican principles, Milton retorted as follows in his *Second Defence for the People of England*:—'In my blindness I enjoy, in no inconsiderable degree, the favour of the Deity, who regards me with more tenderness and compassion in proportion as I am able to behold nothing but Himself. Alas! for him who insults me, who maligns and merits public execration! For the divine law not only shields me from injury, but almost renders me too sacred to attack; not, indeed, so much from the privation of my sight, as from the overshadowing of those heavenly wings, which seem to have occasioned this obscurity.'

It is worthy of remark that in addition to the eighteen English and six Italian sonnets, Milton wrote one English sonnet with a tail, *i.e. On the New Forcers of Conscience under the Long Parliament.* During the later periods of Italian poetry this form of the sonnet is frequently to be found, but examples of it are also to be met with almost as early as Dante.

It is worthy of mention that between Milton (who closed the first of the three great periods of sonnet literature) and Stillingfleet (who began the second) there was one poet only (except Edwards and others of no special mark) who kept alive the art. This was Samuel Woodford, a sonnet-writer of no great power, who wrote nine sonnets, four of them being translations.

Benjamin Stillingfleet. — Page 47.

This sonnet was originally printed in the *Preliminary Observations on the Sonnets* in Todd's second edition of Milton, 1809, where the editor adduces it as proving how attentively and how suggestively Milton was studied and imitated seventy years after his death.

'The author of this sonnet, the grandson of Bishop Stillingfleet, was well known in the literary assemblies which Mrs. Montagu, Mrs. Ord, and Mrs. Vesey made so famous soon after the middle of the last century, and from him the "Blue Stockings" derived their title, for Stillingfleet's stockings being of that colour, Admiral Boscawen called the assembly of these friends the Blue Stocking Society.'—JOHN DENNIS, *English Sonnets.*

Thomas Gray. — Page 48.

'It will easily be perceived, that the only part of this sonnet which is of any value is the lines printed in italics (6th, 7th, 8th, 13th, and 14th); it is equally obvious that, except in the rhyme, and in the use of the single word "fruitless" for fruitlessly, which is so far a defect, the language of these lines does in no respect differ from prose.'—WORDSWORTH, Preface to *Lyrical Ballads.*

It seems curious that Wordsworth should have encountered so much rancorous abuse for the above, and one other similar criticism. The passage quoted might, if taken alone, be open to the charge of hypercriticism, but taken in connection with the essay which it was designed to illustrate, it is in all respects generous and even laudatory. Wordsworth's purpose was to prove that the language of a large portion of every good poem, even of the most elevated character, must necessarily, except with reference to the metre, in no respect differ from that of prose, when prose is written well; and hence Gray was quoted as one who had attempted to widen the space between prose and verse by a curious elaboration of poetic diction, but whose works nevertheless were extreme examples affording proof enough that there neither is nor can be any essential difference between the language of prose and metrical composition. Of quite another kind (and perhaps deserving of the critical outcry against Wordsworth's note) is Coleridge's criticism in the *Biographia Literaria*, where Gray's sonnet is accused of incongruous imagery which confounds the real thing with the personified representation of the thing, and of employing neither the language of prose nor that of good sense.

Line 11. So in the MS., now in the possession of Mr. Archibald Constable, Edinburgh. *Seek* has hitherto been printed for *seize*.

Anna Seward merits recognition if only because of her wise and generous defence of Chatterton. At a time when the memory of the author of so fine a poem as *The Ballad of Charity* (and perhaps nothing comparable to it of its kind was written in the eighteenth century) was being hounded out of public respect by the men who personified all existent literary mediocrity, Miss Seward spoke up heartily and unfalteringly for the unfriended 'whelp' whose works were 'the most extraordinary products' that had 'encountered' the huge lexicographer's 'knowledge.' The spirit of her ungrudging tribute was so wholly free from all trace of contemporary bias that what she said to so much purpose might have been written within our own time by Mr. Masson, Mr. Skeat, or *The Quarterly Review* (July 1880). She says:—

'Though Chatterton had been long dead when Johnson began his *Lives of the Poets*,—though Chatterton's poems had been long before the world—though their contents had engaged the *literati* of the nation in controversy; yet would not Johnson allow Chatterton a place in these volumes in which Pomfret and Yalden were admitted. So invincible were his grudging and surly prejudices—enduring long-deceased genius but ill, and contemporary genius not at all. That Cowper also had paid no attention to Chatterton's writings, "of which all Britain rung from side to side," appears from his assertion that Burns, whose beautiful compositions seem to have been forced upon his notice, was the only poet since Prior's time whose composition stood in no need of allowance from the recollected obscurity of birth and education. He must have heard of Chatterton, and if he wanted all generous curiosity to look into his verses, he had no right to make such an assertion, disgraceful to himself, and unjust to the greatest genius, his early extinction considered, which perhaps the world ever produced.'

But Chatterton has at length taken his place among the English poets. Professor Skeat's admirable modernisation of the Rowley poems, together with the selection recently published in Mr. T. H. Ward's series, affords evidence and to spare of his title to the tardy distinction. Chatterton no longer asks indulgence on the ground of his humble extraction or education; and as to the alleged immaturity of his genius, it may be doubted if one or two of his best passages yield in poetic favour, breadth of conception, power of thought, insight into character and knowledge of the world, to anything by any man whatever.

It is a circumstance not sufficiently known, that Keats's original dedication to *Endymion* stood thus: 'To the Memory of the most English of Poets except Shakspeare, Thomas Chatterton;' and no definition could be more exactly and exhaustively to the purpose than this.

William Wordsworth. — Page 56.

Surely the spirit of this wonderful poem is most deeply representative. To one whose life is spent amidst Nature's solemn solitudes where, in that hour in which night melts into dawn, the rook's or raven's cry makes the stillness yet more still, this wistful outlook on the vesture of the great heart of the sleeping city brings a sense of awe, even greater than that which comes when the craggy promontories, far from the broil of the busy multitude, seem to quiver under the first grey of daybreak that leans down upon them in their loneliness. And to one whose life is spent in London, who loves it, owes it half his joys and all his sorrows, such a picture as Wordsworth has added to the number of things unmatchable in English poetry, cannot but bring a feeling that must almost express itself in tears.

Page 57.

'He (Wordsworth) does not search his mind for subjects; he goes forth into the world and they present themselves. His mind lies open to nature with an ever-wakeful susceptibility, and an impulse from without will send it far into the regions of thought; but it seldom goes to work upon itself.'—SIR HENRY TAYLOR. It may be doubted if anything whatever has been said to more purpose than this by Sir Henry Taylor in denoting the quality and limitations of Wordsworth's genius, though many theories have been formulated which make pretension to more philosophical accuracy. . . . *An impulse from without will send it far into the regions of thought; but it seldom goes to work upon itself.* How true this is may be tested by using it as a critical gauge upon almost any page of Wordsworth's work. Even the great Ode, which from its nature must be a creation of more or less spiritual origin, obtains its primary impulse from a purely concrete view of external change, and is apparelled throughout in garments that belong to the earth. Wordsworth seems to have been conscious of the limitations of his genius. He believed that he had never known any one but himself who had a true eye for Nature, one who thoroughly understood her meanings and her teachings; and it is manifest from his eulogy of Frederick Faber, who had pointed out to him effects on the mountains, which with all his great experience he had never detected, that as a lover of Nature he set a price on nothing higher than the gift (in which the shepherd and the mariner all the world over were probably as rich as he) of noting her changeful moods. Doubtless he would have regarded with suspicion a temperament which held with Nature a more spiritual intercourse, and hence perhaps his lifelong distrust of Shelley.

An impulse from Nature would send his mind far into regions of thought, and cause it to generate moral ideas which, as Matthew Arnold says, he could make applicable to life. But no touch of natural phenomenon had power to make him lose that sense of isolation from Nature, which because of his human individuality became to him a chasm that might not be passed. Wordsworth never delved out of the abyss of being one strong emotion. He was more dependent upon the promptings of his eye and ear than Keats himself. In the full deep sense of the phrase, he was the most sensuous great poet of his period, for three at least of his contemporaries—Coleridge, Shelley, and Keats—were rich in spiritual minds that could go to work each upon its own vision. His one gift, however, of pushing up into a spiritual atmosphere incidents which were in themselves quite mundane, he possessed in a degree higher than all others, and no better example of it could be desired than the sonnet on page 57,—a thing which (separated from the moral ideas associating with it) is a descriptive work so tenderly and serenely felt that it falls on the ear like a prolonged, unheard, spiritual *Hush!*

Page 59. In the first edition this sonnet is headed London, 1802, and appears to have been written on the declaration of peace with France under the Consulate. It should be read together with the sonnet following, and with the sonnets dated October 1803. It is almost peculiar to Wordsworth's objective sonnets that an historical thread runs through them which, as a recent writer shows, almost affixes a date to each.

Page 61. 'Note the repeated recollections of Spenser here (*Colin Clout's come home againe*, 245):

"Triton, blowing loud his wreathèd horne."

Line 248 introduces Proteus, and 283 ends with "pleasant lea." Wordsworth's penultimate line recalls Milton also (*Paradise Lost*, vol. iii. p. 603):

. . . "and call up unbound
In various shapes old Proteus from the sea."'

D. M. MAIN, *Treasury of English Sonnets.*

Page 62. Henry Reed, in his spirited and admirable lectures on poetry published in Philadelphia, 1857, prophesied that Wordsworth's sonnets would be the last of his works to gain very general favour. The exact opposite is the fact, and the acute critic is seen to have made at least one bad shot for the truth. Any reader who is at the pains to trace through periodical literature the notable reviews of Wordsworth's work which have been published since the early volume of Descriptive Sketches will have no difficulty in perceiving that the sonnets are the only part of that work which has from the first received universal approval. In those early notices of the *Edinburgh Review*, which are now by general ascription attributed to Jeffrey, the sonnets were repeatedly eulogised as examples of what noble work the author could achieve when his self-constituted code of laws as to diction became from any cause inoperative. As to the full scope of Wordsworth's poetic canon, there has throughout been considerable misapprehension, in which so sympathetic and penetrating a critic as Coleridge himself is found to have shared. Wordsworth's first purpose was to cut out of credit the overdressed fashion of language, the millinery, ribbons, drapery, false flowers, gold lace, not to speak of soiled frippery, which disfigured a literature given up to 'conscious swains,' 'nymphs,' 'Phœbus,' and 'the fair.' All this was to be done by the substitution of the language of real life—the chastened language of prose. Now, the early efforts to this end chanced to deal with homely subjects, and the public, headed by the *Edinburgh Review*, at once concluded that the language of *humble* life was the diction intended by the new poetic sect to take the place occupied by the elaborate and pointed language of the followers of Pope. Hence the prolonged outcry against simpleness and silliness. But language to Wordsworth was to be indeed the body and sensuous phenomenon of thought, which when it rose to exalted subjects should find expression in majestic phrase. The great Ode and then the sonnets followed to prove that the same directness of chastened real life diction, which had been used in the plains of every-day rustic experience, was to be employed on a level of intellectual and emotional elevation. But critics did not see that in Wordsworth's view the language of Alice Fell and the language of Milton were equally the language of real life, only at opposite poles of experience.

'The only military enterprise set on foot during the year's peace, if we except the occupation of Switzerland, was the expedition to St. Domingo, . . . where whites and mulattoes had commenced a civil war, and the negroes had also asserted their rights. The latter being most numerous gained the ascendancy, headed by a chief of inflexible character and of such high talents, both for warring and ruling, as to merit the name of the black Buonaparte. Toussaint L'Ouverture, such was his name, had established his rule in St. Domingo. It was as beneficent and vigorous as that of the first consul in Europe; but the latter was determined to recover the island. . . . The blacks, after making a stubborn resistance, were subdued, and the chiefs compelled to submit. Most of them accepted command under the French, except Toussaint, who scorned the offer, and merely demanded to return to his farm. . . . Toussaint was seized, sent on board ship, and conveyed to France, where he lingered many years.'—CROWE, *History of France in Cabinet Cyclopædia.*

Samuel Taylor Coleridge. — Page 66. 'This sonnet is very characteristic of the rich indolence of the author's temperament. The very toning of the rhymes is as careless as the mood in which he is indulging.'—LEIGH HUNT.

Page 67. This sonnet, most masterly in its way, requires some explanation of its origin and aim. It appeared first in a series of three sonnets in an early number of the *Monthly Magazine*, and was signed NEHEMIAH HIGGINBOTHAM. The year of its publication (1797) affords a clue to its significance. In that year appeared the *Poems* published by Coleridge, Lamb, and Lloyd. Viewed in relation to this volume, the sonnet given above is seen to be one of three clearly satirical of the several peculiarities of the joint authors. It is intended to ridicule the indiscriminate use of lofty and inflated language and imagery by bringing such swelling diction into ludicrous associations. We have only to remember that Coleridge alone of the authors in question was addicted to this form of literary excess, and to observe that the phrases employed are entirely borrowed from Coleridge's earliest work, in order to assure ourselves that this sonnet is designed to be satirical of Coleridge's own imperfect method. To satirise himself anonymously was surely one of Coleridge's best pleasures, only less relishable to him than to acknowledge a satire after it had been mistakenly attributed to an enemy or falsely claimed (with much show of mock reluctance) by a quasi-friend. In a note to the *Biographia Literaria*, Coleridge reprinted this sonnet with a frank statement of its genesis, but offered no explanation of the uses intended to be served by its fellows. Silence in such a case is significant, and puts us upon a right trace of interesting inquiry touching the personal relations of Coleridge and Lamb. It is known that an estrangement divided for a time these fast friends, but of the occasion of quarrel only the most conjectural explanations have hitherto been made. Now it is on record that Lamb loved his sonnet-muse with infinite tenderness, charged Coleridge when compiling their joint volume to spare his 'ewe lambs,' and even went the length of passionately defending certain of his offspring from Coleridge's strictures. The characteristic defect of Lamb's sonnet-work in his early solemnly-serious days, was an affectation of great simplicity, for which *simpleness* would have been perhaps a fitter name. Upon this Coleridge (for once exercising his satirical gift on a friend—surely the next most pardonable thing to exercising it upon himself) brings his whole battery of banter to bear. This is Coleridge's sonnet satirical of Lamb:—

To Simplicity.

O! I do love thee, meek simplicity!
  For of thy lays the lulling simpleness
  Goes to my heart, and soothes each small distress,
Distress, though small, yet haply great to me!
'Tis true, on lady fortune's gentlest pad,
  I amble on; yet, though I know not why,
  So sad I am!—but should a friend and I
Grow cool and miff, O, I am very sad!
And then with sonnets, and with sympathy,
  My dreamy bosom's mystic woes I pall;
Now of my false friend 'plaining plaintively,
  Now raving at mankind in gener-al,
  But whether sad or fierce, 'tis simple all,
All very simple, meek SIMPLICITY!

The result upon the author satirised was almost the reverse of what might have been looked for in the case of the writer who was soon to be the generator of the essays of the bantering Elia. The authorship of the three sonnets in the *Monthly Magazine* was probably known both to Lamb and Lloyd, the latter of whom took early occasion to leave Coleridge's house, where he had lodged, while the former addressed to Coleridge on the eve of his departure for Germany a most biting letter of masked good-will on general topics, not directly dealing with their private connections. The letter (given in Cottle's *Recollections*) is, beyond question, one of the subtlest and most penetrating examples of irony extant, and it is astounding that the friendship of Coleridge and Lamb could ultimately have survived it. This is Lamb's letter:—

'THESES QUÆDAM THEOLOGICÆ.

'*1st*, Whether God loves a lying angel better than a true man?

'*2d*, Whether the archangel Uriel could affirm an untruth, and if he could, whether he would?

'*3d*, Whether honesty be an angelic virtue, or not rather to be reckoned among those qualities which the schoolmen term *Virtutes minus splendidæ*?

'*4th*, Whether the higher order of Seraphim illuminati ever sneer?

'*5th*, Whether pure intelligences can love?

'*6th*, Whether the Seraphim ardentes do not manifest their virtues by the way of vision and theory; and whether practice be not a sub-celestial and merely human virtue?

'*7th*, Whether the vision beatific be anything more or less than a perpetual representment, to each individual angel, of his own present attainments, and future capabilities, somehow in the manner of mortal looking-glasses, reflecting a perpetual complacency and self-satisfaction?

'*8th and last*, Whether an immortal and amenable soul may not come to be condemned at last, and the man never suspect it beforehand?

'LEARNED SIR, MY FRIEND,—

'Presuming on our long habits of friendship, and emboldened further by your late liberal permission to avail myself of your correspondence, in case I want any knowledge (which I intend to do when I have no *Encyclopedia* or *Ladies' Magazine* at hand to refer to in any matter of science), I now submit to your enquiries the above theological propositions, to be by you defended or oppugned (or both), in the schools of Germany, whither, I am told, you are departing, to the utter dissatisfaction of your native Devonshire, and regret of universal England; but to my own individual consolation, if, through the channel of your wished return, learned sir, my friend, may be transmitted to this our island, from those famous theological wits of Leipsic and Gottingen, any rays of illumination, in vain to be derived from the home growth of our English halls and colleges. Finally wishing, learned sir, that you may see Schiller, and swing in a wood (*vide* poems) and sit upon a tun, and eat fat hams of Westphalia,

'I remain,

'Your friend and docile pupil, to instruct,

'CHARLES LAMB.'

The letter was in truth an atrocious outrage inflicted in punishment of such a playful offence, and Coleridge is said to have appeared greatly hurt by it, and to have handed it to Cottle, saying, 'These young visionaries will do each other no good.' Assuredly such an epistle was calculated to shatter that belief in Lamb's gentleness, which led to Coleridge's naming him 'the gentle Charles.'

One further conjecture as to the personal relations of these writers (though yet more open to question) may be worthy of mention. It is known that when Coleridge produced his *Christabel*, and all the notable critics and most of the poet's friends were unanimous in the extraordinary opinion that the second part was the 'best nonsense poetry yet written,' Lamb was wont to say that the noble passage on the separated friends was enough to redeem it. Now, is it not probable that Lamb believed the passage had a personal significance, and thought he guessed the secret of it? The great body of the second part of the poem was written about 1808, but is it not possible that this portion of it was written at the time of the quarrel? Nay, when we note the clumsy joining up of the reference to Sir Leoline and Roland at the close of it, we are bound to believe that the passage in question had once a separate existence. The 'House that Jack Built' is worthy of insertion on its own merits, worthy of being remembered because it seems to play a part in the lives of two memorable men, and worthiest of attention because it is a reasonable conjecture that but for its existence and the existence of its fellow sonnets, that passage of *Christabel* would never have been written, which has excited almost from the first the admiration of every lover of great poetry.

To make this note complete, I append the sonnet satirical of Lloyd, but owing to the obscurity of that author's work, the points of caricature are to a large extent lost to us. The facts relating to Lloyd's connection with Coleridge are so far forgotten, that it needs to be said that he was a young man of literary taste, who had been introduced to the poet during the period of residence at Bristol, and who (conceiving a passionate admiration of his genius) obtained permission to lodge with him—contributing no doubt materially to the expenses of the household.

Pensive, at eve, on the hard world I mus'd,
  And my poor heart was sad: so at the moon
  I gazed, and sigh'd, and sigh'd! for ah! how soon
Eve darkens into night! Mine eye perus'd
With tearful vacancy the dampy grass,
  Which wept and glitter'd in the paly ray;
  And I did pause me on my lonely way,
And mused me on those wretched ones, who pass
O'er the black heath of sorrow. But, alas!
  Most of MYSELF I thought: when it befel
That the sooth SPIRIT of the freezy wood
  Breath'd in mine ear—'Ah this is very well;
But much of *one* thing is for *no-thing* good.'
  Ah! my poor heart's inexplicable swell!

Charles Lamb. — Page 69. There is a sonnet by Lamb which is akin to this in spirit, and called 'Leisure.'

'O darling laziness! heaven of Epicurus! Saints' Everlasting Rest! that I could drink vast potations of thee thro' unmeasured Eternity—Otium *cum* vel *sine* dignitate. Scandalous, dishonourable, any kind of *repose*. I stand not upon the *dignified sort*. Accursed, damned desks, trade, commerce, business. Inventions of that old original busybody, brain-working Satan—Sabbathless Satan. A curse relieves: do you ever try it?'—LAMB to MISS BETHAM, 1815.

Page 70. One scarcely needs the external evidence which is available in order to recognise in the foregoing touching portraiture the features of a face that recalls as sad and tragic a life as literary biography bears record of.

'The best in the English language.'—COLERIDGE. 'In point of *thought* the sonnet stands supreme, perhaps, above all in any language.'—LEIGH HUNT. Joseph Blanco White. Page 71.

This sonnet appeared first in the *Bijou*, 1828 (Pickering).

One fatally disenchanting line in the sonnet appears throughout all the interminable controversy provoked by it to have escaped attention:—

'Whilst fly and leaf and insect stood revealed.'

It is enough to account for the foregoing being the author's only sonnet except one, to note the poverty of vision which did not see that *fly* and *insect* are here synonyms.

It is right that this sonnet should be published. It bears no relation to the foregoing example in strength and splendour of conception, but it is quite as admirable in point of technique, and contributes towards the formation of a just, if moderated, estimate of the author's place among sonnet-writers. Page 72

Written at Hampstead, December 1816, in competition with that on the same subject by Keats. Leigh Hunt. Page 75.

This magnificent sonnet, which hitherto finds a place in one only of our sonnet anthologies, was, like the foregoing sonnet, written in friendly rivalry with Keats, and also, it is now certain, with Shelley. The most jealous asserter of Keats's incomparable superiority over Hunt as a poet will not grudge a frank confession of the latter writer's absolute mastery in this instance. I doubt if English sonnet literature contains any other such solemn and perfect realisation of the awe that steals over us when the soul of man is brought face to face with the great mystery of time. The personification embodied in this powerful and direct utterance is beautiful and faultless. The octave opens in slow and all but breathless accents, and closes with a swift resonant *boutade* that seems to send the blood dancing to the finger-tips. Observe then the change of tone at the opening of the sestet; but to me the last lines of the whole are feeble and dispiriting. Leigh Hunt's reputation as a poet may be said to be scarcely commensurate with his genius,—a result due no doubt in some Page 76 measure to the early brutal criticism of his *Rimini*, and to the fact that he outlived the men who could have defended his personal character from the foul aspersions cast upon it in relation to that poem. Perhaps if Hunt had died with Keats, Shelley, and Byron, between 1820 and 1830, instead of surviving Wordsworth, he, like them, would have been amongst the English poets to-day.

The following are the sonnets *To the Nile* written by Keats and Shelley:—

Son of the old moon-mountains African!
  Stream of the Pyramid and Crocodile!
  We call thee fruitful, and that very while
A desert fills our seeing's inward span:
Nurse of swart nations since the world began,
  Art thou so fruitful? or dost thou beguile
  Those men to honour thee, who, worn with toil,
Rest them a space 'twixt Cairo and Decan?
O may dark fancies err! They surely do;
  'Tis ignorance that makes a barren waste
Of all beyond itself. Thou dost bedew
  Green rushes like our rivers, and dost taste
The pleasant sun-rise. Green isles hast thou too,
  And to the sea as happily dost haste.

John Keats.

Month after month the gathered rains descend
  Drenching yon secret Ethiopian dells,
  And from the desert's ice-girt pinnacles
Where Frost and Heat in strange embraces blend
On Atlas, fields of moist snow half depend.
  Girt there with blasts and meteors Tempest dwells
  By Nile's aërial urn, with rapid spells
Urging those waters to their mighty end.
O'er Egypt's land of Memory floods are level
  And they are thine, O Nile—and well thou knowest
That soul-sustaining airs and blasts of evil
  And fruits and poisons spring where'er thou flowest.
Beware, O Man—for knowledge must to thee
Like the great flood to Egypt, ever be.

Percy Bysshe Shelley.

'Much more congenial with Wordsworth in spirit, . . . and more closely allied to him in manner than the general body of the sonnet-writers of his time was his young friend, Sir Aubrey de Vere, a poet who, amidst the political excitement of the Reform period, in which the bulk of his poetry appeared, attracted little notice from his contemporaries, but whose merits have met a more fitting appreciation in the succeeding generations.'—*Dublin Review*, January 1877.

Sir Aubrey de Vere.

Page 79.

Mr. Swinburne considers this one of the author's noblest and completest poems. Though of a different class of diction, it recalls forcibly the spirit of Wordsworth's sonnet on Toussaint, and a third example could hardly be quoted so much in harmony with either. Bonnivard was imprisoned by the Duke of Savoy for his defence of the Genevese against the Piedmontese tyranny.

Lord Byron

Page 81

'There is a sort of literary insincerity about Barry Cornwall's verse that found no counterpart in the beautiful character of Mr. Procter. We wonder at rapturous addresses to the ocean

"I'm on the sea! I'm on the sea!
I am where I would ever be."

from the landsman who could never, in the course of a long life, venture on the voyage from Dover to Calais, and at bursts of vinous enthusiasm from the most temperate of valetudinarians; but the poet would have defended his practice by his own curious theory, that "those songs are most natural which do not proceed from the author in person."'—EDMUND W. GOSSE, *The English Poets*, vol. iv.

Bryan Waller Procter.

Page 83.

It may, perhaps, be permitted to an ardent Shelleyan, even in a time of unexampled Shelley-worship, to say that the sonnet does not appear to have been a form of composition adapted to the genius of this poet. A certain high quality of beauty one does assuredly recognise in the example here given, whereby to identify the great genius-hand, as well as a certain strength of conception which must needs have gone with the work of one who was never under any conditions of poetical restraint a

Percy Bysshe Shelley.

Page 84.

weakling. Mr. D. M. Main (in all respects an admirable editor) has printed the five stanzas of the *Ode to the West Wind* as a series of sonnets. Indeed they are barely to be called even stanzas—the poem is terza rima, but to divide it into sections is to reduce terza rima to quasi stanza-work. Surely this is an act which has no better effect than to cripple the matchless fashioning of the finest lyric Shelley achieved, in order to endow that author with a number of imperfect sonnets.

John Hamilton Reynolds.

Page 90.

Reynolds acquires an interest from being the friend and correspondent of Keats, and the brother-in-law of Hood. It was in answer to him Keats wrote his 'Blue, 'tis the light of heaven,' and to him, also, Keats addressed his *Reminiscence of Claude's Enchanted Castle*. The sonnet given in the text appears to be inspired by Keats's *Isabella*, but assuredly the author is not open to the charge of imitating his friend too slavishly. Indeed, the marvel rather is that so much social amenity between the two writers could have co-existed with so little intellectual affinity. Reynolds wrote a whimsical medley called *The Fancy*, dealing with pugilism and kindred matters from a fantastic point of view, and containing three rather vigorous sonnets on 'pet' pugilists of the day. The following is the best example:—

Sonnet on the Nonpareil.

With marble-coloured shoulders, and keen eyes
  Protected by a forehead broad and white,
  And hair cut close lest it impede the sight,
And clenchèd hands, firm and of punishing size,
Steadily held or motioned wary-wise
  To hit or stop,—and 'kerchief too drawn tight
  O'er the unyielding loins to keep from flight
The inconstant wind that all too often flies,—
The Nonpareil stands. Fame, whose bright eyes run o'er
  With joy to see a Chicken of her own,
  Dips her rich pen in claret, and writes down
Under the letter R, first on the score—
  'Randall, John; Irish parents; age not known;
Good with both hands; and only ten stone four.'

This was published in 1820, under the pseudonym of Peter Corcoran. As a serious poet Reynolds is disappointing, although the sonnet in the text (taken from his *Garden of Florence* volume, published under the name of John Hamilton), has points of tender beauty. Reynolds contributed frequently to the *London Magazine*, but usually anonymously. A really graphic article on the trial of Thurtell is by him. He wrote the well-known *Peter Bell the First* on the strength of Wordsworth's advertised poem, and was joint author with Hood of *Odes and Addresses to Great People.* A sonnet without rhymes (probably a draft), but full of splendid colour, was, in addition to the sonnet already mentioned, addressed by Keats to him.

Another friend of Keats's, Charles Wells, was a sonnet-writer, but his one known sonnet (*To Chaucer*) falls short of that rank which a consensus of opinion would demand of the author of *Joseph and his Brethren.* Structurally it is irregular, being, indeed, in scheme of rhyme no more than a stanza of five heroic couplets, headed by a quatrain containing an intermediate couplet. Robert Herrick and Frances Kemble have sonnets similarly constructed. To Wells the sonnet 'As late I rambled in the happy fields' was addressed by Keats, three years after whose death the great Scriptural drama appeared, under the pseudonym of H. L. Howard. Much valuable information touching the career of this author appeared at the time of his death in *The Athenæum*. *The Academy* at that period published a pregnant notice by Mr. E. W. Gosse, wherein it was stated that, discouraged by the cold reception of his two published works, Wells burnt large quantities of unpublished MSS. This statement is doubted by certain of the author's connections; but R. H. Horne, who knew him well, and had, at an early date, seen in progress manuscript tragedies of various kinds which seem wholly lost, thinks it only too probable. There is a note extant (not, to my knowledge, yet published), showing how cheerful in his last illness Wells was even to the end. It states that his son, 'the eminent engineer,' was present with others, and that they at one moment thought Wells certainly dead, when he suddenly revived, and said quite cheerfully, 'Ah! you thought I was gone, but you see I am not leaving you yet.' The cause of quarrel between Wells and

Keats is known to the few surviving members of their circle, but this (as it touches upon a thoughtless practical joke) had perhaps better be left unpublished.

William Cullen Bryant.

Page 91.

Hartley Coleridge has a sonnet on *November* in his 'Sonnets on the Seasons,' but it lacks the pathos of this by Bryant; it has, however, much homely play of sportive fancy, as--

> 'Yet still at eve we hear the merry owl,
> That sings not sweetly, but he does his best.'

To my view there is nothing more conspicuous in Bryant than the influence of Wordsworth; and this sonnet, though Shakspearean in structure, is essentially Wordsworthian.

John Keats.

Page 96.

Keats wrote exactly fifty sonnets, of which exactly twenty appear worthy of him. Perhaps hardly any other of his is quite so perfect as this, though the subject (deeply representative) seems at first sight unimportant. But who has not felt the like despair of youth? The eleventh and twelfth lines are purely in the spirit of Shakspeare. Indeed, without being Shakspeare's, they are Shakspeare absolute.

Page 97.

The singular mis-rhyme in the fourth line seems to echo curiously a line in *Endymion*—

> 'So sad, so melancholy, so bereft.'

A poetic tribute in sonnet-form came to Keats at Teignmouth, from some anonymous admirer of *Endymion*, who coupled it with the gift of a £25 note. The story and sonnet are alike worthy of remembrance, if only as affording evidence of the cordial appreciation with which the poem was received in unknown quarters, outside the circle of the 'Cockney School.' In the course of a letter to his brother and sister (dated by Lord Houghton 1818-19), Keats says incidentally: 'I forgot to mention, once more, what I suppose Haslam has told you, the present of a £25 note I had anonymously sent me.' After this he passes at once to other affairs, but a page or two further on reverts to the matter thus: 'I will now copy out the sonnet and letter I have spoken of.' (He has not spoken of them at all.) 'The outside cover was thus directed, "Messr. Taylor & Hessey, booksellers, 93 Fleet Street, London," and it contained this: "Messr. Taylor & Hessey are requested to forward the enclosed letter by some *safe* mode of conveyance to the author of 'Endymion,' who is not known at Teignmouth; or, if they have not his address, they will return the letter by post, directed as below, within a fortnight: Mr. P. Fenbank, P. O., Teignmouth, 9th November 1818." In this sheet was enclosed the following, with a superscription:—"Mr. John Keats, Teignmouth;" then came "Sonnet to John Keats," which I could not copy for any in the world but you, who know that I scout "mild light and loveliness," or any such nonsense, in myself:

Star of high promise! Not to this dark age
  Do thy mild light and loveliness belong:
  For it is blind, intolerant, and wrong,
Dead to empyreal soarings, and the rage
Of scoffing spirits bitter war doth wage
  With all that bold integrity of song:
  Yet thy clear beam shall shine through ages strong,
To ripest times a light and heritage.
And those breathe now who dote upon thy fame,
  Whom thy wild numbers wrap beyond their being,
Who love the freedom of thy lays, their aim
  Above the scope of a dull tribe unseeing,
And there is one whose hand will never scant,
From his poor store of fruits, all thou canst want.

I turned over and found a £25 note. Now this appears to me all very proper; if I had refused it I should have behaved in a very braggadocio dunderheaded manner; and yet the present galls me a little, and I do not know that I shall not return it, if I ever meet with the donor, after whom to no purpose have I written.'

Prince, a Lancashire poet of whom Dr. Lithgow has written a memoir, has the following sonnet on *Endymion*, in which the mellifluous sweetness of the greater singer is creditably reproduced :—

On Receiving the Poems of Keats from a Friend.

Thanks for the song of Keats—as rich a boon
As ever poet unto poet sent:
Oh! thou hast pleased me to my heart's content,
And set my jarring feelings all in tune.
'Twere sweet to lie upon the lap of June,
Half hidden in a galaxy of flowers,
Beneath the shadow of impending bowers,
And pore upon his page from morn till noon.
'Twere sweet to slumber by some calm lagoon,
And dream of young Endymion, the boy
Who nightly snatched a more than mortal joy
From the bright cheek of the enamoured moon.
Thanks for the song of Keats, whose luscious lay
Hath half dissolved my earthly thoughts away.

Page 99. This sonnet was written in 1819. All we know definitely of its origin we learn from a journal-letter written to his brother and sister-in-law somewhere between 19th March and 15th April 1819. He says:—'I am afraid your anxiety for me leads you to fear for the violence of my temperament, continually smothered down; for that reason, I did not intend to have sent you the following Sonnet; but look over the two last pages, and ask yourself if I have not that in me which will bear the buffets of the world. It will be the best comment on my Sonnet; it will show you that it was written with no agony but that of ignorance, with no thirst but that of knowledge; when pushed to the point, though the first steps to it were through my human passions, they went away, and I wrote with my mind, and, perhaps, I must confess, a little bit of my heart. . . . I went to bed and enjoyed uninterrupted sleep; sane I went to bed, and sane I arose.' It seems impossible to say exactly at what period Keats was first assailed by the malady which from the beginning he knew to be fatal, but it is certain that when this sonnet was written he had already received premonitions of his death-warrant, and knew that of the ten years he had yearned for, in which to overwhelm himself in poesy, only a meagre moiety would be allowed to him. He had accepted with an appearance of resignation the fate which in his eyes forbade that he should leave an immortal work behind him; but the agonies of his inner life were not less but more because he seemed to put by all hope of the deed which his soul had decreed, and to pass quietly to that sterner future wherein his youth must grow pale and spectre-thin and die. We know he did not grudge his friends his society even at that period in which he had most melancholy occasion for isolation (see page 257 of Lord Houghton's *Life and Letters*), and when the fretting influences of his encroaching malady made him a victim to some groundless suspicion, and more than naturally perceptive of actual injury, and sensitive to its sting. For a time after the certainty possessed him that he must die, he was wont to join cordially as before in the gathering of friends, laugh when others laughed, and hide under a cheerful bearing the sure consciousness of his approaching end. I take it (notwithstanding the letter quoted) that it was after an evening spent in such fashion that, returned to his solitary room, and alone with his own heart only for questioned and questioner, he cast off all restraint, and wrote this sonnet. His over-wrought nature could bear no further tension. *Why did I laugh to-night?* He knows now how short is the whole lease of his life: his fancy can compass the utmost limit of life's possible joys. Tortured with the presence of unattainable world-ensigns, his pride has no resource but to hold them in contempt. Better to be half in love with easeful Death, to call him soft names, to cease upon the midnight without pain, for Death is more than Fame or Beauty, it is more than Life, because it is Life's recompence. *I say, why did I laugh?* No voice can make response.

I well know that to direct attention to this side of Keats's mind is to run the risk of being tabooed by those persons who stigmatise as ill-bred the smallest sympathy with any manifestation of a mind that is not at all times outwardly contained and decorous enough to be presented at court, apparelled always in the full pink of a pretty propriety. That Keats should continue to prove endurable to exalted natures who sit superior to all emotion over which they cannot exercise restraint, must be a baffling mystery to one who does not see that such persons have had need to account to their tranquil maturity for the spontaneous sympathies of what must seem to them their earlier and too responsive years. The recent mistaken efforts to lift Keats to a high level of stoical personal character are acquiring certain ludicrous aspects. It was enough, surely, that with the best possible purposes Lord Houghton should seek to establish an argument for Keats's absolute indifference to adverse criticism, and to do so in the teeth of the unquestioned circumstance that *Hyperion* remained unfinished because of the coldness of the reception given to *Endymion*. But it is yet more astonishing that other writers (after disposing of certain excrescences, which they regard as the legacy of the apothecary's apprentice) should seek to prove that the true basis of the nature of the poet in his higher moods was a great spirituality, to which sensuality could establish but remote alliance. Of course, it may at once be said that spiritually Keats was no weakling, that he was fast rising out of his Paradise of Sensation into his Paradise of Mind, but with his loving yearning after loveliness he seemed always to have a look southwards, and his whole nature, saturated in sentient sensuousness, seemed to follow the sun constantly. Why, then, can we not take him as he is, without digging beneath the surface of his work for a spirituality never consciously hidden there? It is one thing to wrest him from the unwise worshippers who exalt their 'lovely and beloved Keats' for those qualities which are least in him, and quite another thing to ignore his perfect hold of that sensuousness which is a treasure no true artist may forego.

Page 100. Compare the following with lines 6 and 7 :—

The ocean heaves resistlessly
  And pours his glittering treasure forth ;
His waves—the priesthood of the sea—
  Kneel on the shell-gemmed earth
And there emit a hollow sound
  As if they murmured prayer and praise.

DAVID VEDDER.

About Keats there is nothing marvellous or miraculous, if by such we mean simply that which is beyond the natural. No startling development ; no morbific transfiguration ; only easy evolution ; devout endeavour ; loyal purpose ; the *gradual growth* of a mind that was great and healthful.

We cannot see more clearly to what perfectness the artistic method of Keats was fast attaining than by glancing at the evidence his sonnets afford of his progress. The fine one on Chapman's *Homer* came early, it is true, as also did the fanciful one on Chaucer's *Flower and Leaf;* but these two came leashed with many a sorry draft such as no judicious lover of Keats will grieve much to find omitted from this collection. Later came *The Day is Gone*, *As Hermes Once*, *Why did I laugh? To Homer*, and, lastly, *Bright Star*. These later sonnets prove indisputably that Keats's method was maturing, because breaking away from the disproportion which was at the beginning his characteristic defect. Assuredly no warning voices whispered fears that Keats's genius would have known the blight that comes of prematurity, even if his body had resisted the tendency to decline that was born with it.

Hartley Coleridge.

Page 104

The following, on the same subject, has qualities of beauty. It is by William Henry Cuyerl Hosmer:—

O Night! I love thee as a weary child
  Loves the maternal breast on which it leans!
  Day hath its golden pomp, its bustling scenes;
But richer gifts are thine: the turmoil wild
Of a proud heart thy low, sad voice hath stilled,
  Until its throb is gentler than the swell
Of a light billow, and its chamber filled
  With cloudless light, with calm unspeakable:
Thy hand a curtain lifteth, and I see
  One who first taught my heart with love to thrill,
  Though long ago her lip of song grew still:
A strange mysterious power belongs to thee,
  To morning, noon and twilight-time unknown;
  For the dead gather round thy starry throne!

'To see him brandishing his pen,' a friend of Hartley Coleridge has written, 'and now and then beating time with his foot, and breaking out into a shout at any felicitous idea, was a thing never to be forgotten. . . . His sonnets were all written instantaneously, and never, to my knowledge, occupied more than ten minutes.'

Some of the happiest, and all but the earliest, of my recollections are associated with the beautiful vale in which Hartley Coleridge made his home; and many half-pathetic half-amusing stories I remembered to have heard there concerning that wayward poet of promise, from lips now silent as his own. In addition to the above description of his habits while in the throes of composition, I recall one similar description, which goes to show in what curious fashion he sometimes took his pleasures in poetic pains. Fifteen years ago there lived on the western side of the lake at Grasmere an old farmer who had been in his youth a companion of Hartley Coleridge, and I remember that he would point out a croft of his, and describe, with infinite zest, how the crazy little poet was wont to run round it in mad and breathless haste, pausing at intervals to jot down something on the fly-leaf of the book he carried in his hand, then starting off afresh at yet greater speed, and keeping up this extraordinary literary exercise (for at such times he was believed to be under the influence of his muse) for an entire hour, equally oblivious of the broad-mouthed merriment of the rustics who had congregated on the road that bounded the field on the high side, and of the amazement of the gentler strangers who rowed on the lake beneath.

Poor Hartley, with all his waywardness (nay, perhaps, by reason of it), was beloved by the peasantry, amongst whom there still remain traditional anecdotes illustrative of that generousness of his which knew no limit until it reached a point that concerned chiefly his personal welfare. I have seen tears start to the eyes of one who knew him, when recounting how he would run to save a child from the anger of its parents, and clasp a donkey around its neck to guard it against a cudgelling. He was perennially impecunious, yet never murmured at his poverty: happy when he possessed anything, and could spend it with the first congenial soul he met; and when his temporary affluence subsided, happy still; miserable only in those great moments of inspiration in which the sense of his abject and forlorn condition came freighted with the full weight of remorse. Amongst his neighbours he was accredited with a marvellous gift of improvisation, and one sonnet of his hitherto unpublished, and now (together with inedited scraps of various kinds) placed at my disposal, seems to afford evidence of such a faculty. One night, forty-three years ago, Hartley, then in his accustomed convivial mood, was wagered to be able to write 'straight away' a sonnet on any subject to any given set of rhymes. The subject chosen and the rhymes selected (the manuscript shows the rhyme-words in a distinct hand), the poet produced the following, writing, an eye-witness tells me, as fast as the pen would flow:—

Oh, when I have a sovereign in my pocket
  I cannot sit, my toes extempore dance
  Gay as a limber son of merry France;
'Tis like grey hair enclosed in gilded locket
Whose gold and glass by contrast seem to mock it.
  So momentary riches will enhance
  The pride of Poverty; so high advance
The hopes of man; but soon, alas! a docket
Misfortune strikes: the obliterating sponge
  Of fell reverse makes all our joys exhale.
Shall I in ocean take a fatal plunge?
  Or shall I with sixpennyworth of ale
Condole the sovereign spent? or get quite friskey
And just Hibernify myself with whiskey?

The sonnet cannot possibly do injury to the fame even of so great a sonnet-writer as the author at his highest assuredly was, and certainly it affords evidence of extraordinary facility when judged of in relation to the conditions under which it was produced. My guess is that the second and third lines contained a humorous significance for the dalesmen, from the circumstance that there lived amongst them a little French dancing-master to whom the popular love of the poet was a cause of jealousy. It is equally true of Hartley as of his father, that he was conspicuously wanting in continuity of purpose, and touching his consciousness of this weakness, I remembered to have heard that when at a time shortly after the death of S. T. C., Hartley was occupied in hanging a picture somewhat high on the walls of his room in Nab Cottage, the bottom of the chair on which he was standing gave way, and he slid between the stiles to the ground; whereupon the irresolute little poet recovering himself, exclaimed: 'Ah! how I wish my poor father could see me now; he said I could never get through *anything*, but I've certainly got through *this*.' One other hitherto unpublished sonnet may be acceptable here:—

AMBLESIDE FAIR, 1845.

What a huge turmoil in a little town;
  Swell'd like a cow that has been eating clover;
  See thievish Mercury, suspended over
Each canopied stall, and eager to pounce down;
I see the maid that has not learned to frown—
  From service free, no mistress to reprove her—
  Hangs on the arm of him she deems her lover;
God grant he is no worse than honest clown.
Among the crowd I see a scarlet coat,
  That would seduce the lad to other arms
Than such as thine on which he seems to doat.
  Oh, gentle maiden, work with all thy charms;
Let not thy chosen youth make thee the wife
Of man whose psalmody is drum and fife.

By the side of the beautiful Rotha, within three paces from the grave of Wordsworth, Hartley Coleridge (not without detractors in his day) awaits with the greater singer the final dawn when all shall be united who have been apart. To me, whether from association or sympathy, no spot on earth can be more sacred than that little churchyard among the mountains.

Happily the sonnet-work of this author has in recent years obtained such cordial recognition that there remains no longer the necessity to dwell upon its excellence. It is true that the influence of his father's genius is not easily discernible in Hartley Coleridge's sonnets. The profound and all but unexampled reverence which the son manifested did not go the length of inducing an imitation of the inflated language and imagery which disfigured at times the father's sonnets,—a disproportion almost as remarkable between the two as is the father's superiority to the son in all other forms of verse. It is also true that the influence of Wordsworth's genius is observable in Hartley's best poetry, but the false poetic diction which the elder poet made it his business to banish was not more unlike the language of real life which he sought to substitute, than the impassioned and majestic flow of that great body of sonnets which he wrote in confessed imitation of Milton was unlike the subtle sweetness of the most felicitous part of the work of the younger writer. What strikes us to most purpose as the truly individual side of Hartley Coleridge's genius is the profound yet simple pathos, the soft and touching, indeed all but indescribable suggestion of baffled purposes, of hopes half realised, of loves slipping away—and in all this patient, tranquil, and resigned self-delineative spirit his sonnets gravitate towards the tenderness, pathos, and introspection of the sonnets of Shakspeare. One living poet of genius greater than his own he does in the more solemn of his utterances recall. The sonnet given on page 105 is fraught with something of the sense of spiritual overthrow, which gives such profound significance to Rossetti's *Lost Days*, and similar sonnets in *The House of Life*, while it is wanting in the vividness of sustained vision which imparts to those sonnets a place amongst poems that peal in our ears like cries wrung out of the heart at some terrible moment.

In his caustic letters to Bowles, Byron asserted Pope's superiority to Wordsworth by maintaining that the followers of the one had obtained rank amongst poets of distinction, whilst those of the other had taken fit places as proven imbeciles. It is needless to say that the facts being granted (and they were certainly open to sober question), the deduction was wholly illogical, indeed amusingly irrational. It is nevertheless true that a poet's followers may help materially to quicken or serve seriously to retard the acknowledgment of his genius, and in this respect it was well for Keats that so soon after him came so true a poet as Hood, whose early volume of verse contained so many derivative points from his works. There is noticeable in the sonnet given on page 108, a more contained adequacy of conception than Keats ever quite achieved, a maturity of craftsmanship which Keats had scarcely attained to in sonnet work (perhaps because his sonnet genius had more to mature), and an absence of the disproportion which was Keats's early defect, together with a freedom from the many-coloured prismatic brightness of phrase which ultimately gave place to the directness which came of contained and disciplined purpose. But the essential poetic attitude of mind is the same here and in Keats's sonnets, and this is no unworthy offspring of the archangelic muse which gave us that master's noblest work. It may reasonably be doubted if English sonnet literature contains anything finer on the subject; and in this connection arises the reflection that poets who (whilst above the degree of minor poets) have never ranked with the highest, have written certain of the noblest poems in this form. It may be that the arbitrament of rigid structure, while it acts as a trammel upon poetic temperaments so fervent as to crave licence to outride it, serves as a spur to the invention of less imaginative minds. Hence perhaps the occasional superiority of Drayton, Donne, Hartley Coleridge, and Hood, over Spenser, Shelley, Byron, and Coleridge the elder. Of course only the highest impulse under the severest discipline has availed to produce such masterpieces as Shakspeare's sonnet on Lust (perhaps the first of the five or six greatest of all English sonnets), Milton's on the Piedmontese Massacre, Wordsworth's composed on Westminster Bridge, Keats's on Chapman's *Homer*, and Tennyson's on Montenegro.

Sir Henry Taylor. — Page 114.

This is the dedication to Philip van Artevelde.

Benjamin Disraeli (Lord Beaconsfield) — Page 115.

This sonnet, which appears to have been first printed in Mr. Ramsay Forster's Catalogue of the Stowe Collections, and in *Notes and Queries* for May 19, 1855, was written by Disraeli when on a visit at Stowe, and was suggested by a silver statuette of the Duke of Wellington. The collections were dispersed in 1847; the sonnet must belong to a period somewhat earlier than that. The following is said to be the only other sonnet written by Lord Beaconsfield:—

On the Portrait of the Lady Mahon,[1] 1839.

Fair Lady! thee the pencil of Vandyke
  Might well have painted; thine the English air,
  Graceful yet earnest, that his portraits bear
In that far troubled time when sword and pike

[1] Mahon is the junior title of Stanhope. The original of the portrait is now the Dowager Countess of Stanhope.

Gleamed round the ancient halls and castles fair
  That shrouded Albion's beauty; tho' when need
They too, the soft withal, could boldly dare,
  Defend the leaguered breach, or charging steed
Mount in their trampled parks. Far different scene
The bowers present before thee; yet serene
  Tho' now our days, if coming time impart
Our ancient troubles, well I ween thy life
  Would not reproach thy lot and what thou art—
A warrior's daughter and a statesman's wife.

B. Disraeli.

I think a consensus of opinion would adjudge this at once the noblest of Longfellow's sonnets, and the most purely characteristical. Whether in sweet and equable phrase or adequacy of completed conception, it must, I think, be accorded the first place among the sonnets of American authors.

'A noble sonnet, but the last distich is inferior to my

And Ocean 'mid his uproar wild
Speaks safety to this Island child.

Ode to the Departing Year.

'I notice this only because it is too inferior for the resemblance. The parenthesis is weak and of an alien tone of feeling: a *μετάβασις εἰς ἄλλο γένος*, though I admit not *εἰς ἕτερον*. But it is a noble strain, *non obstante*.'

S. T. Coleridge, *Note on the margin of his copy of Tennyson-Turner's Sonnets.*

Frederick Tennyson, brother of Charles Tennyson Turner, and of the present Laureate, wrote (*Martha and the Holytide*) a series of sonnet stanzas not unlike this sonnet in mood and quality of beauty in his little volume *Days and Hours*, published in 1854.

'The dominant charm of all these sonnets is the pervading presence of the writer's personality, never obtruded, but always impalpably diffused. . . . In his poetic philosophy, Mr. Turner is a disciple of Wordsworth, faithful to the great 'Tintern Abbey' manifesto upon the moral influence of nature, and diligent in reading her as a Sibylline book, fraught with inexhaustible meanings.'—HENRY G. HEWLETT, *Contemporary Review*, September 1873.

Edgar Allan Poe. — Page 126.

This fine poem contains fifteen lines, but is in all other essential particulars a sonnet.

Alfred Tennyson. — Page 128.

This magnificent invocation (worthy of rank with the noblest of Milton's sonnets and the most impassioned of Wordsworth's Liberty series) should be read together with the same author's sonnet on the Polish Insurrection.

Elizabeth Barrett Browning. — Page 133.

If Elizabeth Browning be adjudged worthy to ride in the very van of English sonnet-writers, with Shakspeare, Milton, Wordsworth, and Keats, as an Amazon in noble alliance with these male warriors, her right of rank with the foremost is founded upon claims somewhat dissimilar from those advanced by her great fellows. She has written nothing which quite touches the summits of possibility in sonnet-excellence—nothing matchable with Milton's great sonnet of denunciation, or Keats's of admiration, or the wonderful poem in which Wordsworth condenses the wistful yearning of the modern mind towards exanimate forms and deposed symbols of beauty. But the so-called sonnets from the Portuguese are among the most perfect *series* of love-poems in our language, and it is in the nature of things that a sonnet of the supreme order can rarely be one of an inter-related series, but is oftenest a thing wholly self-inclusive, being the outcome of a special inspiration which is born with it and exhausted by it. Briefly, such a poem is its own be-all and end-all, and as the 'Sonnets from the Portuguese,' by reason of their more or less interdependent character, evade the conditions under which the few paramount examples have been produced, we should perhaps do them the most honour in considering them rather as a single passion-poem or high exposition of Love, for upon this ground they can scarcely admit of precedence. Indeed the world has read no love poetry like unto this, nor ever will until Nature repeats the phenomenon of a truly great poetess; for the 'Sonnets from the Portuguese' are, in the highest sense, essentially *woman's* love-poetry—essentially feminine in their hyper-refinement, in their intense tremulous spirituality, and above all, in that absolute saturation by the one idea, which bears out Byron's familiar dictum that—

> '— love is in man's life a thing apart,
> 'Tis woman's whole existence.'

Whilst this note is passing through the press, I feel constrained to append a word of warm tribute to an exposition of woman's love which appears to me in most respects on a level with the 'Sonnets from the Portuguese' in points of tenderness and resignation, at the same time that it is above them in purity of lyric medium, - I mean Christina Rossetti's series of sonnets entitled 'Monna Innominata,' appearing in her volume, *The Pageant*, 1881.

I don't know whether any one has ever guessed why Mrs. Browning called her sonnets 'from the Portuguese.' It seems to me that (apart from the mere purpose of not fully identifying them with herself) she may have thought of a celebrated series of love-letters, often called 'the Portuguese letters.' They were written by Marianna Alcaforada to Captain (afterwards Marshal) De Chamilly, towards 1665.

The following sonnet, by Dean Alford, is little less beautiful than that given in the text, but much less known :—

EASTER EVE.

I saw two women weeping by the tomb
Of one new buried, in a fair green place
Bowered with shrubs ;—the eve retained no trace
Of aught that day performed,—but the faint gloom
Of dying day was spread upon the sky ;—
The moon was broad and bright above the wood ;—
The distance sounded of a multitude,
Music, and shout, and mingled revelry.
At length came gleaming through the thicket shade
Helmet and casque—and a steel-armed band
Watched round the sepulchre in solemn stand ;
The night word passed, from man to man conveyed ;
And I could see those women rise and go
Under the dark trees moving sad and slow.

Charles Whitehead.
—
Page 147.

This very fine sonnet may be said to be quite unknown. Whitehead wrote the admirable and exceptional novel of *Richard Savage*. Little is known of his life. His first publication was in 1834, and his last, according to Allibone, in 1861. In some of his habits he appears to have been somewhat of a Richard Savage himself. After a career during part of which he was a publisher's reader, he emigrated to Australia, and is said to have died there. There is a sonnet by Henry Kirke White (*To a Taper*) akin to the above in substance, but of course inferior in execution. My guess is that a vivid passage in Coleridge's *Friend* inspired Whitehead's noble sonnet. A subscription edition of Whitehead's poems was published by Bentley about 1848-9; the leading poem is called 'The Solitary,' and is in the manner of Goldsmith; though not widely known, it had had for many years previous a special circle of admirers. A singular contrast to this is afforded by a wild and weird rhapsody in verse entitled 'Ippolito,' contained in the same volume. No other sonnet is there to be found equal to the one given. The reference to 'Ippolito' reminds me that this was a period when the muse occasionally went stark staring mad. About the time of the first publication of 'Ippolito' in an annual, there appeared as a small volume a poem by Thomas Tod Stoddart (the recently deceased authority on angling), entitled, 'The Death Wake, or Lunacy: a Necromaunt in three Chimæras.' Its nature would not be much cleared up if any amount of description were added to the mere title.

Wm. Bell Scott.
—
Page 150.

The *Athenæum* (Nov. 26, 1881) has the following remarks on this sonnet:—'Mr. W. B. Scott, although he has written some admirable sonnets of the objective type, is no doubt at his strongest in such sonnets as "The Universe Void," which, apart from its poetic qualities, seems to have within it as much of mere intellectual energy as any sonnet in the language. This seems a bold statement, but the reader will agree with it on carefully studying the sonnet.'

Mr. Scott's early connection with that movement in contemporary poetry called pre-Raphaelite renders it expedient, perhaps, to give other specimens of his work. The following has a passionate intensity that it would be difficult to surpass:—

PARTED LOVE.

Methinks I have passed through some dreadful door,
  Shutting off summer and its sunniest glades
  From a dark waste of marsh and ruinous shades:
And in that sunlit past, one day before
All other days is crimson to the core;
  That day of days when hand in hand became
  Encircling arms, and with an effluent flame
Of terrible surprise, we knew love's lore.

The rose-red ear that then my hand caressed,
  Those smiles bewildered, that low voice so sweet,
    The truant threads of silk about the brow
Dishevelled, when our burning lips were pressed
  Together, and the temple-pulses beat!
    All gone now—where am I, and where art thou?

And here is a sonnet showing a mastery over mere structural difficulties such as sonnet-writers do not often display:—

A GARLAND FOR ADVANCING YEARS.

Wear thou this fresh green garland this one day,
  This white-flowered garland wear for Love's delight,
  While still the sun shines, ere the west so bright
Fades down into the shadows cold and grey;
Wear thou this myrtle-garland while ye may,
  Love's wings are wings that hate the dews of night,
  Nor will he rest for ever in our sight,
Companioning our gradual western way.

Wear this plain dark-green garland still to-day
  To please Love's eyes, else not for all the might
  Of all the gods, nor any law of right,
Will he content with age's disarray
Let pass him by the youthful and the gay:
  And yet 'twere hard to live in Love's despite.

Mrs. Kemble has written a considerable body of sonnets, but her work is unequal, and many stanzas published as sonnets can show but little title

Frances Anne Kemble.
Page 151.

to the name. In structural transgression, however, she sins in common with Wells, Herrick, and others of yet higher rank. The sonnet given in the text is so powerfully done as to occasion regret that this form of composition has not been more zealously cultivated under the discipline of rigid law by one who has certainly had it within her power to produce one of the noblest sonnet-utterances in the language. I have pointed the sonnet afresh in copying it from the pages of the Magazine in which it appeared.

Aubrey de Vere. — Page 154.

Sir William Rowan Hamilton, late Astronomer-Royal of Ireland, was regarded as the profoundest and most abstruse of modern mathematicians. His earliest work, entitled *On Systems of Rays*, published when he had but emerged from boyhood, was of a character so abstract that, as was affirmed, but a small number of Europe's mathematicians were capable even of reading it. He became subsequently well known through a succession of discoveries in pure science, the most important of which is developed in his celebrated works on 'Quaternions.' Like Leibnitz, he was a man of universal genius, delighting no less in metaphysical speculation and imaginative literature than in mathematics, while, as a linguist, he was very early acquainted with many languages of the East as well as of the West. He was said by Wordsworth to have singularly resembled Coleridge in the character of his intellect. His intimacy with those two great men imparted, no doubt, their high and meditative pathos to the sonnets, of which he left behind a considerable number. He was an eminent example of the well-known fact that, while smaller gifts often generate vanity, and undermine faith, the highest genius is associated with humility and simplicity, with a kindly heart, and a devout spirit. In simplicity he was a child, and in his convictions an earnest and reverential Christian. Sir W. R. Hamilton was born in Dublin, A.D. 1805, and died at the Observatory, Dublin, A.D. 1865.—A. DE V.

Ebenezer Jones. — Page 157.

This sonnet is undoubtedly rugged, but it is also extremely finely felt, in both of which particulars it is on a level with the only other sonnets of this author: *On Eyeing the Eyes of one's Mistress.*

This is the first sonnet-stanza of the poem 'Brother and Sister' which appears in the *Jubal* volume. The ninth and eleventh stanzas are characterised by the same tenderness, but do not admit of isolation.

Roscoe published anonymously in 1851 a tragedy entitled *Violenzia*, of which his biographer (R. H. Hutton, in a Prefatory Memoir to his Poems and Essays, published nine years later) said:—'I do not think any drama, except Mr. Kingsley's *Saint's Tragedy*, which has appeared since the publication of Shelley's *Cenci*, is worthy to be compared to it in power and beauty.'

'In spite of manifest faults, on the side of violence and of occasional obscurity, Dobell seems to us to claim a permanent place among the English poets of his century. Though unequal, his verse at its best is both strong and delicate; his imagery, though redundant, original and incisive. But the great merit of his work is that it is steeped in that higher atmosphere in which all enduring literature breathes and moves.'—JOHN NICHOL in *The English Poets*, vol. iv.

The Honourable S. E. Spring Rice was born in the year 1814, and died in 1855, while on his return from Alexandria, to which he had gone while suffering from pulmonary disease. He was the son of Thomas, first Lord Monteagle, and father of the present Lord Monteagle. For many years he filled the place of one of the Commissioners of Custom, the duties of which office, as well as those of a country gentleman and magistrate, at a later period, he discharged with an energy and efficiency rarely combined with the studious habits and refined literary taste evinced in his sonnets, qualities which rendered him delightful as a companion. He was one of those who laboured most assiduously and successfully in aid of the distressed poor in Ireland during the famine years from 1847 to 1850.

The poems of this author were published in Boston, 1856. The allusion in this sonnet to the Cossack appears to point to the time and incidents of the Crimean War as the period and occasion of it. Boker achieved a great success in his own country as a dramatist by his 'Francesca da Rimini.' His Love Sonnets are Petrarchian in structure, and essentially Shakspearean in substance: they are perhaps his most striking, delicate, plaintive, and picturesque work.

Alexander Smith. — Page 185.

This is a sonnet so singularly akin in spirit and bright and equable phrase to Keats's early sonnet-work, that it seems difficult to believe that it has not strayed somehow out of the pages of the poet who, in 1816-17, wrote such sonnets as 'Give me a golden pen.' Of course it is wanting absolutely in the imaginative ordonnance which gave the later sonnets of Keats their special distinction; but, besides that it has a value of its own, it is interesting as evidence of how attentively Keats was studied. It is worthy of mention in this connection that Thomas Wade, who wrote in the *Tattler* about 1831, and afterwards published his verses in several small volumes, was with Hood amongst the first and most notable of English Keatsians. Wade wrote a great body of sonnets in a volume called *Mundi et Cordes Carauna*, but it is surprising that so much taste and feeling, as his work undoubtedly possessed, could exist with so little positive value. The sonnets convey the idea that, with so much that is good they ought always to be better. Wade dedicated to Charles Wells a poem called *The Contention of Love and Death,* and his best work is *Prothanasea.* His period was about 1835.

Richard Watson Dixon. — Page 195.

Canon Dixon published in youth (1861-1864) two volumes of poems, entitled respectively *Christ's Company and other Poems,* and *Historical Odes and other Poems.* Much in these volumes is replete with religious fervour and mystery, and they also share largely the special mediæval development which was originated in poetry about that date. At the same time, the *Historical Odes* give proof of the largest and sanest spirit in treating national themes. The Ode on the Franklin Expedition is a masterly echo of heroic history. In some of the pastoral lyrics there is an imagery not inferior to that of Keats himself, albeit chargeable with some derivativeness. It must be admitted, however, that these early poetic volumes are unequal in the completeness of their parts to a strange and almost unaccountable degree, when the fulness of their author's culture is considered. Nevertheless, Canon Dixon affords probably by far the most striking instance of a living poet deserving the highest recognition yet completely unrecognised.

William Davies. Page 215

Mr. William Davies's sonnets are here extracted from his volume of poems entitled *Songs of a Wayfarer*, a book absolutely delightful from its delicacy of soul and refreshing cheer. This special mention is here made of the volume on account of its having for so many years missed its due share of public favour. Though often branching into graver moods, it partakes greatly of the spirit of Herrick; and the same may be said even more absolutely of its author's other poetic volume, *The Shepherd's Garden*.

Theodore Watts. Page 217

This exceptional sonnet (deeper and finer, perhaps, in conception than its companion works, if less distinguished by rarely admirable liquidity of phrase) attracted a great deal of attention on account of the novelty of its motive. 'Mr. Theodore Watts's sonnet to "Natura Maligna," wrote an Orientalist in the *Athenæum*, February 5, 1881, is, even in its very epithets, just such a hymn as a Hindu Puritan (Saivite), would address to Kali ("the malignant") or Parvati ("the mountaineer"),

The Lady of the Hills with crimes untold.

It is to be delivered from her that Hindus shriek to God in the delirium of their fear.' I have been tempted to make liberal use of Mr. Watts's sonnets, on account of their striking originality of subject-matter, purity of style and structure, and rigid avoidance of the poetic diction of the day. All, except one, of Mr. Watts's sonnets here given are reprinted from the *Athenæum*, by the editor's kind permission.

Hon. Roden Noel. Page 230.

Written at the time of the Bulgarian massacres, when England was on the point of lending armed support to the Turk against Russia.

Oliver Madox Brown. Page 263.

This is one of the two existent sonnets written by the rarely-gifted young novelist the author of the romance of the *Black Swan*. A great sombre beauty, and passionate, if not chastened fervour, will be seen in it, even by those who doubt if the genius of the writer had yet attained to the maturity that alone can compass truly great sonnet work. Many of the lyrics that came from the same hand are amongst the best of their kind—rich in picturesque phrase, and with cadences as new as they are musical. The prose works have the note of pronounced individuality. The young author died before he had completed his twentieth year, but it would be wrong to say that his writings are at all more interesting by reason of their promise than their fulfilment. He accomplished work that will one day honour him in a high degree. It scarcely needs prophetic vision to foresee a time not far in the future when the name of Oliver Madox Brown will rank with the name of Nathaniel Hawthorne, as that of a romance-genius not less distinctly personal and enduring.

IN a last word, I must make grateful acknowledgment of the indebtedness under which I rest to the many friends who have given me valuable and disinterested help while this volume has been passing through the press. To Miss Mathilde Blind's cordial intercession on my behalf I owe not a few of the noble sonnets by living poets, printed here for the first time. To Mr. Richard Garnett I remain under lasting obligations for the untiring friendliness with which he has throughout made bibliographical references, to which I have not had access. Indeed, to almost every contemporary writer represented in these pages I owe valuable suggestions, of which I have been equally sensible when I have been able to utilise them, and when it has not seemed practicable to do so. I think I have in every instance sought and obtained permission to reprint, the copyright sonnets included; but if by chance this duty has in any case been overlooked, I must rely upon the fellowship of the author concerned to believe that I have not been capable of conscious neglect, and that in a choice between the injury of printing a sonnet without permission, and the much greater injury of omitting one that seemed to me essential to an anthology having pretensions to completeness, I could not in justice hesitate. In the preface I have said that the arrangement of the authors is chronological, and this is strictly so as to dead authors; but I have experienced such difficulty in ascertaining the dates of living poets, that beyond a broad observance of the priority of the older generation, I have made no rigid effort at chronological sequence in the order observed throughout the last hundred pages.

The book has been so long in the press, and has enjoyed the advantage of so much anticipatory attention, that it seems needful to explain that the one circumstance has been in large part due to my anxiety to justify the other. How far the work is worthy of the friendly interest felt in it must remain with the public to say; but I cannot forbear the expression of a measure of personal regret, that long as it has been in my hands, I can keep it there no longer. To collect, to study, and to annotate these sonnets has been to me for many months a source of pleasure, the like of which I can hardly hope soon to enjoy again. The domain of literature devoted wholly to sonnets and sonnet-writers is wider, and of more interest, than can easily be realised by a reader who has not made it for a time his special province. And in this connection it is fitting that I should offer a word of acknowledgment of my obligations to those writers, the benefit of whose labours I have enjoyed. Reference to the numberless essays on the sonnets written prior to our time need hardly be made, but I should be wanting in gratitude if allusion to the essays of living writers were not forthcoming, even in instances in which (as may, I fear, too frequently have been the case) I have felt constrained to differ wholly from the view taken or verdict pronounced. I have found Mr. D. M. Main's *Treasury of English Sonnets* full of scholarly bibliographical data, unerring in all important matters, and only open to question on the merits of the editor's scheme and the nature of his poetic quest. Mr. John Dennis's *English Sonnets, a Selection*, has seemed to me often eminently judicial, and Mr. Samuel Waddington's two little volumes are thoughtful, pleasing, and popular. Mr. Waddington has the merit of being the first to edit the following sonnet by Robert Burns:—

On Hearing a Thrush Sing.

Sing on, sweet thrush, upon the leafless bough;
  Sing on, sweet bird, I listen to thy strain:
  See agèd winter, 'mid his surly reign,
At thy blithe carol clears his furrowed brow.

So in lone Poverty's dominion drear,
  Sits meek Content with light unanxious heart,
  Welcomes the rapid moments, bids them part,
Nor asks if they bring aught to hope or fear.
I thank thee, Author of this opening day!
  Thou whose bright sun now gilds yon orient skies!
  Riches denied, thy boon was purer joys,
What wealth could never give nor take away!
  Yet come, thou child of poverty and care,
  The mite high Heaven bestowed, that mite with thee I 'll share.

With each of these precursors I think I can, though coming latest on their ground, claim to be on terms of appreciative fellowship. Amongst essayists on the sonnet who are not editors also, I have found Mr. William Davies (*Quarterly Review*, January 1873), and Mr. H. G. Hewlett (*Contemporary Review*, September 1873), worthy successors to Leigh Hunt, Charles Lamb, and Alexander Dyce. Mr. Ashcroft Noble (*Contemporary Review*, September 1880) has proved himself a gifted exponent of sonnet-thought and structure, and this volume bears witness to his title to judge of a good sonnet by affording proof of his capacity to write one.

T. H. C.

INDEX IN METRICAL GROUPS.

The purpose of this Index is to afford, at a glance, a comprehensive view of the relative values of the several forms of metrical structure adopted by English writers, by furnishing a table shewing the number and importance of the sonnets in this volume, written on each of the principal models. The Index is divided into three sections—Shakspearean, Miltonic, and Contemporary. A few sonnets refuse to be classified under any of the three heads, and these are thrown into a Miscellaneous sub-division; but, wherever it has been possible to place a sonnet (whatever its minor variations of rhyme-arrangement) under a leading heading, this has been done.

SONNETS OF SHAKSPEAREAN STRUCTURE.

Under this heading are placed all sonnets constructed on the alternate rhyme scheme, whether with interlacing quatrains, as in Spenser, or without the climax in the couplet, as in Keats.

SONNETS OF MILTONIC STRUCTURE.

Under this heading are placed all sonnets in which the rhyme-arrangement is structurally that adopted by Milton (whatever the number of rhymes employed), and in which the thought has one facet only, and is rendered continuously, whether without break between octave and sestet, as in Milton, or with an accidental metrical pause of comma, colon, or period.

SONNETS OF CONTEMPORARY STRUCTURE.

Under this heading are placed all sonnets (whether old or new) in which the metrical and intellectual wave of flow and ebb is strictly observed, and in which the rhyme-arrangement is structurally the same as that adopted by Petrarch.

SONNETS OF MISCELLANEOUS STRUCTURE.

The sonnets in this sub-section are such as do not fall naturally into any one of the three greater groups.

METRICAL FORMS IN EARLY ITALIAN POETS.

To notify the various leading types of the early Italian sonnets (which have been referred to in classifying the English) may not be superfluous.

Fra Guittone D'Arezzo.

This author (perhaps too frequently and specially cited by critics) has 217 sonnets, of which 209 have the octave constructed on an alternate rhyme-scheme similar to that adopted by Shakspeare, except that two rhymes are employed instead of four. Eight of Guittone's sonnets are of the Petrarchian rhyme-arrangement; 158 of them have four rhymes only throughout, and 59 have five rhymes; 2 are of 16 lines.

Dante Alighieri.

There are 80 sonnets attributed to Dante, and no doubt most of these are genuine; 10 of the whole number have the octave constructed on the alternate rhyme-scheme running on two rhymes, the remaining 70 being of the arrangement known as Petrarchian; 52 of them have five rhymes throughout, and 28 have four rhymes; 12 close with a couplet, and 2 are of 16 lines.

Francesco Petrarca.

The series entitled *In Vita di M. Laura* contains 152 sonnets with five rhymes throughout, and 73 sonnets with four rhymes. The other series, *In Morte di M. Laura*, contains 51 sonnets with five rhymes, and 39 sonnets with four rhymes. The variation in all cases is in the sestet only: the octave running uniformly on two rhymes. Several of Petrarch's sonnets have in the octave the alternate rhyme-arrangement adopted in the great body of Guittone's sonnets, and one of them closes with a couplet, but is otherwise regular as to form. Certain exceptional, and wholly irregular, pieces of fourteen lines are found in Petrarch, and these are of the *Ballata* character.

To follow the entire course of the voluminous series of poets preceding Dante might be to overload these indices with foreign matter. Suffice it that they may on an average be said to follow the same proportionate rule as Guittone. It may be well to note that the sonnet printed first in Italian collections, and dated 1200, being by Lodovico della Vernaccia, is of Petrarchian rhyme-arrangement, and has five rhymes.

REST PRAY SLEEP

www.ingramcontent.com/pod-product-compliance
Lightning Source LLC
Chambersburg PA
CBHW030911270326
41929CB00008B/648

* 9 7 8 3 3 3 7 2 7 5 1 4 3 *